THE PREDATOR EFFECT

THE PREDATOR EFFECT

UNDERSTANDING THE PAST, PRESENT AND FUTURE OF DECEPTIVE ACADEMIC JOURNALS

BY SIMON LINACRE

Published in the United States of America by
ATG LLC (Media)
Manufactured in the United States of America

DOI: http://doi.org/10.3998/mpub.12739277

ISBN 978-1-941269-57-2 (paper)
ISBN 978-1-941269-58-9 (ebook)
ISBN 978-1-941269-59-6 (open access)

http://against-the-grain.com

To Elizabeth, with all my love and thanks

CONTENTS

In April 2016, I was invited by Cabells[1] to sit on a panel at the Association to Advance Collegiate Schools of Business (AACSB) annual conference in Boston, USA. I was asked to contribute to a discussion on the threats posed by predatory journals to academic research and publications. At the time, I was well aware of the problems such journals caused, having dealt with their fallout in various roles over the years at Emerald Publishing. There was standing room only in the small venue allotted for the discussion, mainly due to the star-studded panel—not me of course, but for scholarly communications heavy hitters such as Rick Anderson and Jeffrey Beall.

It was my first taste of what was to become an interest, verging on obsession, fueled by a new role at Cabells from 2018 and fascination with the many twists and turns exhibited by predatory publishing behavior. Much of what I came across with predatory journals was hard to understand at first, and I had 15 years of academic publishing experience behind me. Small wonder then that many academics, funders, and higher education professionals found predatory publishing unfathomable. In that case, was there anything that could be done to support them?

Hopefully, this short book will go some way to explaining what predatory journals are, how they were first conceived, and how they have grown to become such an unwelcome part in the fabric of academic publishing. Their history involves many of the key elements of modern scholarly communications—Open Access (OA), citation analysis, publication ethics—but also includes some of the more unsavory aspects of the industry.

Ultimately, the book ends with the aspiration that the predatory phenomenon can be dealt with positively. It is hoped the more people read this book and understand how predatory journals operate, the more the brief success they have enjoyed so far this century will be short-lived.

NOTE

1   Full disclosure: there are several mentions of Cabells and its products in this book. The author was an employee of Cabells from 2018 to 2022.

CHAPTER 1

INTRODUCTION

There are few topics in scholarly communication more controversial—or that arouse more curiosity—than predatory publishing (Tennant et al, 2019). It is now well established that dishonest actors in the field of publishing are systematically deceiving researchers into parting with money for little or no return—though it must be said that some of these authors know exactly what they are doing. The phenomenon of predatory publishing is familiar to many of us as a topic on social media, of course, but also because of the many emails we receive from unknown correspondents asking us to contribute to a journal, book, or conference on topics about which we know nothing at all.

Cabells' *Predatory Reports* currently lists over 16,000 journals (as of May 2022), which it deems to be predatory, with around 1,800 more such journals added each year (Cabells, n.d.). What is driving such huge growth in these academic-style pseudo-journals? As with other black market activities, including such white-collar fraud as taking cash-in-hand payments to avoid paying taxes, it can be difficult to know the scope and scale of predatory publishing. Indeed, it can be a challenge even to define predatory publishing, partly because it is such a shady undertaking, partly because every topic in publishing is open for constant debate. And yet, predatory publishing practices continue to damage scholarly communications by allowing non-peer-reviewed research to be published and contaminating the academic record.

Even so, predatory publishing practices are now a part of our daily experience.

Most published authors receive spam emails regularly from journals they've never heard of seeking their latest papers, while legitimate publishers must fight predatory adversaries to properly publish articles. In some cases, publishers even have to fight to preserve their own digital identity when a pseudo-publisher hijacks their journals and publishes papers in their name. While the overall shape of predatory publishing may be rather blurred around the edges, the specifics of its impact on authors, funders, and universities are often seen in very sharp focus indeed.

But how did such bad actors enter into the superficially genial world of academic research and publishing in the first place? What we will see in the following chapters is a coming together of new business models, a push for openly accessible research, and a market with unique features that combine to provide the perfect scenario for predatory behavior to proliferate. The history of predatory journals started with the internet, which in turn opened up possibilities for Open Access publishing of academic articles. Once a new business model of paying for the publication of those articles became established, a market was also created to hoodwink authors into publishing for a low price but without the checks and balances afforded by legitimate publishers— and so predatory journals were born. This practice has grown since the early 2000s alongside the growth in Open Access, resulting in the identification of thousands of predatory journals.

What we will also see is that the only "fault" for the current state of affairs lies at the doors of the predatory publishers themselves and the authors who take advantage of their journals to increase their publication numbers. But having said that, there is a huge amount of naivety exhibited by most authors, universities, and governments that has also significantly contributed to the problem.

LIGHT AND SHADE

The aim of this short book is to shed light on the dark arts of predatory journals. Readers will learn about the history and development of predatory journals, their typical makeup and modus operandi, and how to use this knowledge to avoid the traps predatory publishers lay for them. This briefing will not try to define predatory publishing too precisely nor try to measure the value of the enterprise too exactly. It will certainly not seek to identify every guilty agent by name, which would be a lengthy undertaking in its own right. I hope, however, to provide some important contextual information on the topic, as well as some practical guidance and suggestions for authors who are worried about publishing unwittingly in predatory journals (with a specific "Q&A" section dedicated to this concern at the end of Chapter 8).

In writing this book, it is hoped most of the issues concerning predatory publishing are at least brought together in one place. The chapters of this book will present the various aspects of what makes up predatory publishing. Furthermore, the book will

- analyze the various definitions of predatory journals over time;
- review the history of some specific predatory journals—some of which go back to the 1980s and even earlier—and assess the impact of the emergence of online publishing, which enabled the development of the first successful predatory journals;
- explore the differences between subscription and Open Access publishing models, including allowing us to debunk the myth that Open Access journals are somehow inherently predatory;
- assess the impact of Jeffrey Beall on predatory publishing and scholarly communications in general, including the influence of Beall's List before and after it was shut down in 2017;
- estimate of the size of the predatory publishing industry, with particular attention to the Federal Trade Commission judgment in 2019 against OMICS International;
- try to understand why authors publish in predatory journals, including the structures and incentives that may influence certain author behaviors, as well as why certain author communities are more influenced than others;
- offer a step-by-step guide for authors that will allow them to identify the tactics employed by predatory publishing operators; and
- conclude with an examination of the technology and strategies that have allowed predatory journals to be successful and how scholarly communications and academic research stakeholders are adopting

new processes and digital solutions that may help thwart predatory publishers in the future.

Predatory journals have proliferated during the first two decades of the new millennium for several reasons: the development of the Open Access publishing model; the explosion of effective email marketing techniques; and the "publish or perish" incentive structure in which so many academics work. Yet, to truly understand how predatory publishing works, one must examine both the motives and methods of predatory publishers and the motives of authors who submit articles to predatory journals. What are these authors thinking? Why do they submit to these dubious journals? Don't they know that submitting to these journals is unethical behavior that could result in severe sanctions? Predatory publishing has become one of the hottest topics in scholarly communications impacting numerous different stakeholders. It is only when we gain further insight into both the hunters and the hunted that we will be able to act appropriately to solve one of the major problems to have blighted scholarly communications in recent times.

CHAPTER 2

SO, WHAT IS A PREDATORY JOURNAL?

Defining predatory journals has proven to be rather problematic, and the reason for this lies in the term "predatory" itself. While having a perfectly functional definition in the literal sense—"A predatory animal kills and eats other animals" (Cambridge, 2021)—in scholarly communications it is used in the metaphorical sense, which is more intangible—"A predatory person or organisation tries to get something from someone else" (Cambridge, 2021). This definition is illuminating for two reasons. First, it introduces the notions of theft and deceit, which are key factors in any assessment of what predatory publishing entails. And second, it illustrates why defining the practice presents such a problem in an academic context. If academic research is about the pursuit and establishment of truth, how is it possible to prove an attempt at theft, or measure the level of deceit?

In this chapter we will look at various attempts to define the phenomenon of predatory publishing in terms of both academic research on the topic and more pragmatic analysis of what so-called predatory journals do to deserve such a name. If we accept that predatory journals can and do exist, it may be possible to build a more nuanced set of profiles that help create a complex but fully formed picture of what a predatory journal looks and acts like. Whether clearly defined or not, predatory journals have been talked about since the late 2000s and been in existence since at least the 1990s, so agreeing at a basic level what essential characteristics they share will help discussions in the rest of the book as to their history, development, threat, and possible future for scholarly communications.

WHAT IS A JOURNAL?

Before we start trying to categorize predatory journals, it probably makes sense to define what a journal is in the first place. According to *The Business of Scholarly Publishing* (Greco, 2020), the first journals in 1665 were created to be "a usable journal that published research studies and theories in the physical sciences and mathematics." The growth of journals was slow, with only about 1,000 being published in 1929 (Greco, 2020). However, the rate of growth since then has been exponential, with Scopus indexing over 25,000 journals across all disciplines in 2020.

A quick online search of "what is an academic journal" picks up some familiar themes: a journal is a periodical; it publishes at least once a year; it is curated by an editor or editorial team; it includes research articles, commentary, and data written by experts in a given field; content is peer reviewed; published articles are a matter of record; articles are of good quality. It is hard to argue with many of these; however, it feels an all-encompassing definition might be both clumsy and inevitably miss out an important ingredient.

For the purposes of discussion, therefore, the following definition from Wikipedia not only is open-ended and practicalbut also has the virtue of being accessible to most people:

> An academic or scholarly journal is a periodical publication in which scholarship relating to a particular academic discipline is published.
>
> (Wikipedia, accessed May 27, 2021)

PREDATORY JOURNALS: EARLY SIGHTINGS

We'll see in the next chapter more details on the history of journals and the role predatory journals have as a subset of this entity, but for now we will focus on attempts to define the latter. The person, and to an extent the definition, who has become almost synonymous with predatory journals is Jeffrey Beall, the former librarian at the University of Colorado in the United States, who through his writings, investigations, and eponymous list of predatory journals and publishers focused a huge spotlight on their activities.

Beall is credited with both coining the term "predatory journals" and defining them as part of the inclusion criteria for Beall's List. The first use of the term "predatory" appears in a number of articles published in the *Charleston Advertiser* in 2010 (Beall, 2010a; Beall 2010b), where he analyzes several journal publishers that appear to use predatory tactics to lure academics into paying article processing charges (APCs) to publish their articles as Open Access. In these early articles, Beall identifies characteristics such as low-price points for APCs, inflated commitments on behalf of the publishers, and the development of websites that appear to copy those of legitimate journals.

These and other characteristics were used to form Beall's List, a list of journals and publishers that Beall described on the blog site as "potential, possible, or probable predatory scholarly open-access publishers" (Beallslist. net, accessed 03 Jun 2021). The site was shut down in early 2017, but numerous other sites have sprung up purporting to variously archive, update, and amend Beall's original work. We will discuss this work and Beall's impact in Chapter 5, but for the purposes of how predatory journals and publishers have been defined, Beal was quoted in an article in *Nature* that predatory publishers showed "an intention to deceive authors and readers, and a lack of transparency in their operations" (Butler, 2013). Prior to this, he himself had written a news article published by *Nature* where he described predatory journals as "counterfeit," seeking to "exploit the open-access model in which the author pays. These predatory publishers are dishonest and lack transparency. They aim to dupe researchers, especially those inexperienced in scholarly communication. They set up websites that closely resemble those of legitimate online publishers and publish journals of questionable and downright low quality" (Beall, 2012b).

These articles and Beall's preliminary investigations heralded the first appearance of predatory journals in the academic consciousness, but was Beall the first person to recognize them? Certainly, many academics may have thought something fishy was going on when they, like Beall, started to receive unsolicited emails into their inboxes in the 2000s. Perhaps the first person to write about this was journal editor and academic blogger Gunther Eyesenbach in his post "Black Sheep among Open Access Journals and Publishers" (Eyesenbach, 2008). In this post, Eyesenbach described the "spam" emails now familiar to anyone who has any kind of research record and how annoying these unsolicited bulk emails were becoming. Handing out "spam awards," Eyesenbach identified both the key modus operandi of predatory publishers and the factors that led to their success in soliciting for article submissions, such as flattery of the recipient and the need for authors to publish articles in a "publish or perish" regime. Together with Beall, we can see therefore that a fairly clear idea of what predatory journals were and how they operated had emerged by the early 2010s, even if a satisfactory definition had yet to emerge.

TOWARD A DEFINITION

Following the early work of Beall and Eyesenbach, as well as the increased familiarity researchers had with spam emails and online discussions on the topic, more people started to become engaged with the phenomenon of predatory publishing. Naturally, this led to the desire for some researchers to try and understand the topic more and, being academics by nature, try to define the activity and undertake research to further the academy's understanding.

Perhaps the most seminal—and certainly one of the most cited—articles to appear on the topic were published by Shen and Björk in *BMC Medicine* in 2015. The article—" 'Predatory' Open Access: a longitudinal study of article volumes and market characteristics"—was an attempt to quantify the extent to which predatory journals had infiltrated mainstream scholarly communications, and the numbers it reported must have shocked many of those first readers:

- Estimated 8,000 active predatory journals
- Increase in publications in predatory journals from 53,000 in 2010 to 420,000 articles in 2014
- From 2012 publishers with under 100 journals were beginning to gain the largest market share from larger publishers
- Distribution of the publishers' countries and authorship was highly skewed toward Asia and Africa, with three quarters of authors
- APC of $178 (US) per article.

In order to try and size the market for predatory journals, the authors had to try and define what market was. In order to do this, they borrowed Beall's "counterfeit" characterization, as well as his data from the substantial lists that Beall had built up by 2014 for both predatory journals and publishers. However, like other researchers to come they sought to question the term "predatory," suggesting "pseudojournals," which had been used by another author (McGlynn, 2013), and broadening out the process of definitions to include criteria, again using Beall's work (Beall, 2012c). Shen and Björk also recognized the impact predatory journals were starting to have on scholarly communications and academic authors, saying that the journals "have caused a lot of negative publicity for OA journals using APCs, partly due to the spam email that they constantly send out to researchers and partly due to a number of scandals involving intentionally faulty manuscripts that have passed their quality control. . . . This indirectly makes it more difficult for serious OA journals to attract good manuscripts and get accepted to indexes such as Web of Science" (Shen and Björk, 2015).

So, by the mid-2010s, individual authors and the scholarly publishing industry at large were perhaps getting a clearer idea of what predatory journals were, how they operated, and what impact they were starting to have. It was at this stage in early 2017 that Beall's List was shut down, while shortly afterward Cabells announced the development of its *Journal Blacklist* (now named *Predatory Reports*). As more and more studies started to emerge on predatory publishing activities, perhaps the most comprehensive definition was published in 2019 by a team of authors who used a conference on the issue of predatory publishing to come to a consensual definition (Grudniewicz et al, 2019). Using the Delphi process to come to an agreement, the definition the conference settled on was as follows:

> Predatory journals and publishers are entities that prioritize self-interest at the expense of scholarship and are characterized by false or misleading information, deviation from best editorial and publication practices, a lack of transparency, and/or the use of aggressive and indiscriminate solicitation practices.
>
> (Grudniewicz et al, 2019)

This definition, while missing references to peer review that both Beall and Cabells have used in their criteria, did have the advantage of stating what predatory journals and publishers were and probably aligned with many academic authors with some knowledge of their activities. But as we shall see, some take issue with the word "predatory" and indeed extend the characterization of predatory to some of the major academic publishing houses. While in recent times the identification of predatory publishing practices has become better understood, we are still some way short of arriving at an agreed definition.

This is due in part to some quite varied interpretations of what predatory publishing is, definitions that depend on the impact it has on various academic stakeholders. For example, some people argue that large, established subscription journal publishers such as Elsevier are predatory due to a perception of high subscription process and aggressive commercial behavior. In a blog post following the publication of the Grudniewicz et al definition in *Nature* in December 2019, Professor Björn Brembs from the University of Regensburg in Germany concluded after running Elsevier's operations through the five "tests" included in the definition that "so as far as this exercise goes, at least one of the main legacy publishers fits the five criteria for being branded a 'predatory' publisher" (Brembs, 2019). Others have expressed the view that predatory journals as commonly identified are not a problem at all. They say that they offer an outlet for valid but insignificant research or that their activities are relatively small and have little or no impact on scholarly communications. As such, not only are definitions of predatory publishing difficult to agree on but so are the interpretations of the concept in the first place.

A DEFINITION FOR EVERYONE

While it is in important to understand criticisms of predatory journal definitions and challenges that the phenomenon even exists to any meaningful extent, it is also important to accept that for many academics and users there is a real and active problem in the way some publishers lie about the credentials of their journals in order to deceive authors into parting with funds to publish their articles. The validation for this interpretation is provided by the 2019 judgment from the Federal Trade Commission against OMICS Group Inc., a large Open Access publisher (often known as OMICS International or just OMICS) that was deemed to not deliver the publishing services authors had a right to expect after paying their APCs and was fined $50.1 million as a result (Federal Trade Commission, 2019). As we will see when we look at the decision in more detail in Chapter 6, whether a definition of predatory publishing can be agreed on or not, it is very clear that the phenomenon exists and has a detrimental impact on the authors, funders, and institutions involved.

In summary, then, if we take a step back to look at all the definitions and characteristics cited by those tracking the emergence of predatory publishing since the late 2000s, we can establish a workable and straightforward definition for the purposes of this book as follows:

> Predatory journals are deceptive and often fake, giving the appearance of legitimate peer-reviewed journals and impact academic stakeholders by exploiting the Open Access model while using misleading tactics to solicit article submissions.

While there may of course be exceptions to this summation, we should at least be able to grasp the essential characteristics of what predatory journals are and how they operate.

In order to have predatory journals, however we choose to define them, we must have journals in the first place. Journals have been around in some form or the other since the mid-17th century, when journals in the UK and France were published for the first time in 1665. While looking very different to the journals of today, these early periodicals nevertheless shared key similarities—officially recording and disseminating findings from the latest scientific research of the day. While the purpose of academic journals hasn't changed, there have been two major developments that, in hindsight, enabled predatory journals to appear. In this chapter, we will look at the impact of the first of these factors, namely the advent of the internet and how it has transformed scholarly communications. In the next chapter, we will see how this transformation—in addition to the adoption of the Open Access model—created the fertile conditions for predatory journals to flourish.

JOURNALS IN THE 20TH CENTURY

Growth in the number of journals was impressive in the 1900s following a transformative century in the decades before. The science historian Alex Csiszar reports that it was only really in the 1800s that academic societies began to insist on referees reviewing submitted manuscripts (Csiszar, 2016), and then it was done as much for the need for public accountability as it was for independent adjudication of research. In terms of numbers, as we saw in Chapter 2, Greco reports that there were only about 1,000 journals published in 1929 (Greco, 2016). Looking deeper into Greco's investigations, he cites reports saying there were about 500 journals in 1918 and 1,500 in 1939. So, between the Great Wars the growth in the number of journals available to researchers was steady if unspectacular. If this rate of growth had been maintained, we might expect to see around 6,000 or so journals today, instead of the tens of thousands that do exist.

Greco points to the establishment of the United States as a major research superpower after World War II and as one of the stimulants for the exponential growth in journals in the late 1940s and 1950s (Greco, 2016). In addition to this we have seen increased investment in higher education in the shape of new universities and larger budgets, greater focus from governments on scientific research and innovation, and a more commercial approach to journal publishing. This commercial focus saw publishers reap dividends by increasing the amount they published, both in terms of articles and number of journals.

This entrepreneurial zeal was embodied by Robert Maxwell, a British publishing tycoon who would go on to own one of the UK's biggest newspaper publishers. Earlier in his career he established the book and journal publisher Pergamon as a global force, ramping up journal numbers using aggressive marketing and editor recruitment tactics (Buryani, 2017). This resulted in much higher number of journals, which had other publishers scrambling to match in order to remain competitive and not lose too much market share of publishable research. This competition continued into the 1960s and 1970s, with more and more publishers joining the fray and increasing options for the growing number of researchers in universities all over the world. Hierarchies of journals were also established with the introduction of the Impact Factor in the early 1960s in the Science Citation Index (Garfield, 2005), which opened up multiple publication options for authors in the same subject areas, depending on quality—or perceived quality—of the journals. As a result of these activities, journal numbers were propelled ever higher from a succession of factors before the impact of the internet even started to be felt.

JOURNALS MOVE ONLINE

The first journals moved online in the early 1990s, although other forms of electronic platforms were the pioneers in the field. A file transfer protocol

(FTP) server was set up in 1991 to share articles between physics researchers; this later became arXiv.org (Csiszar, 2016), the principal repository for physics research on the internet and copied in many other subjects since then. Nevertheless, publishers soon saw the advantages of publishing article content online so that institutional subscribers could access their journal content online. This move at the end of the century seemed to solve one major problem for libraries that had been building up for the final decades of the 20th century, but also contributed to another major issue at the start of the 21st century—the Serials Crisis and the Big Deal respectively.

We will look at the Big Deal in Chapter 4 in terms of how it developed almost in parallel to Open Access. The Serials Crisis, on the other hand, really started to take shape in the 1980s and 1990s as librarians saw annual subscription prices to journals increase year-on-year, sometimes at above-inflation rates (McGuigan, 2004). The feeling among many librarians and their supporters was that publishers—especially those with high reputation journals—were taking advantage of the fact that university libraries were vulnerable to such regular price hikes. First, this was because some publishers had a virtual monopoly on the top journal in any given area to which faculty members argued vehemently for access. And second, despite the evident costs associated with printing and distributing journal issues all over the world, it was felt publishers were profiteering by increasing subscription prices so much when the actual content and peer review of the journal were provided freely by researchers (McGuigan, 2004).

Online access options, therefore, enabled the market to cool down as publishers could offer subscriptions to many more journals online as a package and reflect the reduction in production and fulfilment costs. The Serials Crisis, however, was far from over, as we shall see in the next chapter. And this "battle" over pricing between university librarians and publishers goes some way to explain librarians' general support for Open Access when it was discussed as a way of offering gratis access to academic research in the early 2000s. It also provides a little background on the views of some librarians and other members of academia who are not as exercised when it comes to predatory publishers, as they see them as perhaps a small price to pay for the gains made in transitioning to Open Access and open science models.

THE FIRST PREDATORY JOURNALS EMERGE

Trying to pinpoint where and when a journal was first published as a result of predatory practices is extremely difficult and may never be truly known. What we do know, as outlined earlier, is that the right conditions were in place to create journals that had a much lower cost base, and therefore lower barriers to entry. The first predatory journals would probably have been experimental, using either existing moribund journals to test out the willingness to pay fees for publication or new journals set up to test the practice with what would have been new e-commerce technology. Some people have tried to identify these first journals, although the work itself is difficult to independently verify. One group has created a website called "Predatory Publishing" and uses Twitter prodigiously under the name @fake_journals to share information and ask for engagement on the topic dozens of times every day. According to their website, they have researched the question of the first predatory journal, believing it to be the *Journal of Biological Sciences* (Predatory Publishing, n.d.). According to the website, the journal was first published by ANSInet in January 2001, and they came to their conclusion following an analysis of 18 publishers first investigated by Jeffrey Beall in four of his earliest papers dating from 2009 to 2012. The journal is still publishing (ANSInet, n.d.) and appears to be a legitimate Open Access journal (with the archive available all the way back to 2001).

So, we can see that there was an Open Access journal publishing in 2001—but was it predatory? Given the difficulties we have already noted in Chapter 2 of defining a predatory journal, it is even more difficult to discern now whether a journal was predatory or not 20 years earlier. And in terms of whether this was the first, it is more complicated by the existence of Open Access journals well before 2001, as well as journals that subsequently became verifiably predatory in nature. The earliest Open Access journal was *New Horizons in Education*, which was originally published by Syracuse University and is now published by Wiley and supported by Florida International University (Wiley, n.d.). This journal began life as an Open Access title in 1987, albeit access was limited due to the limited availability of internet access. However, the oldest journal included in Cabells' *Predatory Reports* database is the *Indian Journal of Aerospace Medicine* published by Scientific Scholar (Indian Journal of Aerospace Medicine, n.d.). The journal states it has published since 1954; however, only two years' worth of volumes (2020 and 2019) is available on the website, and a link to previous volumes going back to 2000 is dead. Another older journal that is included in *Predatory Reports* is the *Journal of Industrial Pollution Control* published by Research & Reviews (a publishing brand used by OMICS International). This title claims to have been published since 1985, and yet only has an available archive going back to 2003—but which is categorized as Volume 19 (*Journal of Industrial Pollution Control*, n.d.).

What we can surmise is that online access enabled predatory-style journals to develop sometime from the 1980s, but at that stage there were little or no means for authors to pay for publication and hence provide a revenue stream for would-be predatory publishers. We will see in the next chapter that the evolution of Open Access models supported by online payment systems could combine with universal online access to create the right conditions for predatory journals to flourish. And what we also know is that whichever journals were the pioneers of predatory publishing, their behaviors were picked up by the likes of Sanderson (2010) and Beall (2009, 2010a, 2010b, 2012a) in their early work, which reviewed these journals' operations and which have lived on to this day. Indeed, some recent research shows that of the 18 publishers highlighted by Beall in those four early papers, 13 are still publishing, with 11 of them increasing their journal output from a decade earlier (Kendall and Linacre, forthcoming). Seven of these are included in Cabells' *Predatory Reports* database, publishing 1,677 journals and representing 11.4 percent of the database (Predatory Reports, retrieved 24 Jun 2021).

It is clear, then, that predatory journals have evolved over a period of at least 20 years and possibly 30 years or more, with key traits remaining part of their makeup through the whole of that time. It is perhaps worth speculating that the evolution of predatory journals—or at least, the avaricious intent shown by those publishers seeking to make a fast buck through deception—had its roots in the postwar expansion of journals by Robert Maxwell and his cohorts. They sought to grow journal numbers as a means to a profitable end and take advantage of a university library system with deep pockets and a desire to provide as much research material as possible for their academic faculty.

It is possibly a little early to refer to their evolution as "history," but the postwar period saw the creation of the commercial publisher that helped identify the industry as a lucrative one, building a platform for what came later. And the 2000s, as a result, certainly saw predatory journals establish themselves as a small but growing part of scholarly communications. This pivotal decade also saw Open Access become a major force in the industry, and one that in due course also became inextricably linked to predatory journals.

CHAPTER 4

SUBSCRIPTION ACCESS VERSUS OPEN ACCESS

The final piece in the jigsaw indicating a paradigm shift in the industry—and for enabling predatory journals to develop—was the advent of Open Access. We have seen from the first few chapters that predatory journals started to develop from certain factors coalescing in the early years of digital publishing. The establishment of the internet and online publishing, a reduction in barriers to entry into publishing, and resentment over ever-increasing subscription prices all contributed to dissatisfaction with the status quo in scholarly communications. Once Open Access (OA) began to emerge as a viable publishing model, all the necessary conditions were in place to allow predatory actors to enter the industry and create an illicit market.

There is a necessary link between OA and predatory journals because (almost) all predatory journals exploit the OA model. But does this mean that OA journals are predatory? This question is often asked, and there is still a widespread belief in some quarters that there is something suspicious about OA journals per se. This misconception—and to be clear, just because a journal happens to be OA does not mean it is predatory or of any worse quality than a subscription journal—is the result of some false assumptions about what OA is, what it is for, and how it has changed the scholarly publishing landscape. So, this chapter will review the emergence of Open Access in the late 1990s and early 2000s and how OA added to universal internet access precluded the rise of predatory publishing.

OPEN ACCESS DEFINED

Open Access as a movement started in the 1990s with the realization that articles could be published online and accessed freely without publishers being involved. Perhaps the defining document of this period is Steven Harnad's "A Subversive Proposal" (Harnad, 1994), an online posting in 1994 that kickstarted numerous discussions about how researchers could make their research available via FTP servers. At the time, publishing research via journals was very much the default path taken by scientists, so to suggest a different route felt almost revolutionary for many people. The key line from Harnad's proposal was as follows:

> If every esoteric author in the world this very day established a globally accessible local ftp archive for every piece of esoteric writing from this day forward, the long-heralded transition from paper publication to purely electronic publication (of esoteric research) would follow suit almost immediately.
>
> (Harnad, 1994)

This discussion carried on throughout the late 1990s with Harnad and several other high-profile figures calling for greater accessibility to research, particularly where that research had been paid for by the taxpayer. This clamor for "Open Access" to research culminated in a number of declarations that sought to define the aims and scope of what had become a movement for change in scholarly communications, as well as defining what Open Access itself meant. In 2002, following a meeting of the Open Society Institute in Budapest, the Budapest Open Access Declaration was made, stating that scholarly work from all disciplines should be openly and freely accessible so it could make its intended impact on the world by self-archiving or publishing in OA journals that had started to appear (2002). A year later, a second statement was made at a similar meeting in Germany called the Berlin Declaration, where a more holistic approach was taken, with calls for governmental and cultural support for OA, and an early attempt to define OA itself (2003).

The Berlin definition set out two conditions for OA: for authors to grant universal use and access to research findings, and for those findings to be made available in at least one online repository. While the full definition sought to be as all-encompassing as possible, it was unable to factor in certain conditions that added layers of complexity. As such, following these initial statements there have been numerous attempts to define OA, all trying to summarize the essence of what the concept actually means to most academics. Perhaps the best definition was put forward by Harvard's Peter Suber, who defined it as follows:

> Open-access (OA) literature is digital, online, free of charge, and free of most copyright and licensing restrictions.
>
> (Suber, 2012)

An even shorter OA definition might be "free to read and free to re-use." However, while these definitions capture the meaning of OA, they are unable to cover the different publication processes involved. For this a color-coded taxonomy has been developed that can help users understand what type of OA is being discussed:

- Gold OA: where an article is published Open Access in a journal, typically following the payment of an article processing charge (APC) by the author
- Green OA: where an article is made freely available online, typically in an institutional or subject repository
- Diamond/Platinum OA: where an article is published Open Access in a journal, and all the costs of publication are covered by a third party, so it is free to the author
- Bronze OA: where an article is published in a journal, and while access is free (at least temporarily) there is no right of re-use.

In terms of predatory publishing, predatory journals are therefore usually Gold OA. Authors are asked to pay an APC for their articles to be published in online journals.

MARKET DYNAMICS

Since the various OA declarations in the early 2000s, Open Access has gradually grown to become a major channel for scholarly communications. If we think about it in terms of market share, in 2000 there was hardly any sharing of research articles outside of the traditional subscription model that had dominated things during the 20th century. However, from almost nothing in 2000 OA articles represented 30 percent of all published articles in 2020 (Pollock and Michael, 2020), and if you include all access types, it was estimated that over half of all journal articles were OA in some way in 2019 (Priem, 2020). In around two decades, OA had gone from an obscure idea to the dominant way research articles were made accessible.

However, what the data from Pollock and Michael also showed was that in 2020, revenues from Open Access publishing were just 7 percent of the total for the publishing industry, less than a quarter of the number of articles published as OA. In other words, while OA has become the norm, revenues still lag far behind subscription access journals. This is not simply because university libraries are canceling journal subscriptions and telling their faculty members to find other ways to access the resources they need (although this has happened, most famously in 2019 when the University of California canceled its subscription to Elsevier (University of California, 2019)). The dynamics of the market have developed so that not only have OA articles started to be published alongside subscription articles in so-called hybrid journals but OA elements are now being included in various "transformative agreements" between publishers and university libraries, which maintain subscription payments while in varying ways allowing for OA publications to be made as part of the deal. As such, these transformative agreements are replacing—or perpetuating—Big Deal agreements that had dominated access arrangements since the 1990s.

PREDATORY SHADOW

Alongside the growth in OA journals and articles in the 2000s and 2010s, predatory journals also increased in numbers. As the payment of APCs became more familiar to authors, predatory journals have been able to deceive authors into believing that they are legitimate journals offering peer review and all the other services undertaken by reputable journals. While Beall identified 18 different publishers in his early work on predatory journals (Kendall and Linacre, forthcoming) publishing over 1,300 journals, Cabells listed over 500 publishers publishing 15,000 journals in 2021 (Cabells Predatory Reports, 2021).

For researchers who don't have any insight into the scholarly communications industry, a journal reflects an opportunity to publish their work, which for many is something their job and career depends on. This lack of understanding has meant authors of legitimate research articles have published in illegitimate predatory journals. One reason put forward to explain how this has happened is that the APC model itself is fundamentally flawed. Dell'anno et al (n.d.) reported that there is no incentive to remove peer review from a subscription journal as that would remove its commercial viability. On the flip side to this, their study showed that up to two-thirds of suspected predatory journals charging APCs accepted articles without peer review, while none of the subscription journals in their sample was guilty of this.

However, it is important to stress that while predatory journals exploit the OA model, there is nothing inherently suspicious about OA journals. For example, a study by Strinzel et al (2019) showed that of the 12,357 journals listed in the Directory of Open Access Journals (DOAJ) in 2018, just 37 of them also appeared in Cabells' *Predatory Reports* (0.3%). Many authors have confused OA with predatory practices as Open Access has grown, and predatory journals have undoubtedly benefited as a result. Indeed, the confusion between OA and predatory journals may have contributed considerably to the success or otherwise of OA journals. In their article on definitions of predatory journals, Krwczyk and Kulczycki (2020), the authors point to overgeneralizations made about OA journals that painted them as predatory in the eyes of some scholars, leading to "unjustified prejudices among the academic community toward Open Access."

In their conclusion, Krwczyk and Kulczycki point the finger at one person as having helped perpetuate the myth that OA journals were in some way part of the predatory journal problem. But this is the very same person who is identified as having done most to alert scholars to predatory journals in the first place: Jeffrey Beall. His name has already cropped up numerous times in the exploration of how predatory journals have developed over time, and in the next chapter we explore his work in more detail.

CHAPTER 5

THE BEGINNING
Beall's Investigations and Beall's List

Jeffrey Beall is the most important individual in the story of predatory publishing so far. There are some shady characters who have published hundreds of journals, and one or two were responsible for the very predatory journals in the early days. But no one is as synonymous with the phenomenon as Beall, or as famous as a result in the scholarly publishing industry. We have already seen he had a part to play in coining the term "predatory journal" and loosely defining what they were. But he also went on to lift the lid on the modus operandi of predatory journals, such as how they used spam emails and false promises to entice submissions from naïve authors. He also framed the discussion of what constituted a predatory journal or publisher, which was often at odds with many people's opinion—especially some of those publishers who found themselves on the famous list.

In this chapter we will look more deeply first at his early research that made his name on the topic and then at Beall's List and the impact the eponymous resource had on academic publishing. Finally, we will look at the legacy of Beall's website after its closure in 2017 and the alternatives that exist today to support researchers in identifying and avoiding predatory outlets. While Beall did a huge amount to shine a spotlight on predatory practices, he was ultimately unable to halt their rise in the 2010s, as we will see in more detail in the next chapter.

PRIVATE INVESTIGATIONS

For most of his career Beall was a librarian at the University of Colorado. He was a prolific scholar, publishing numerous articles and short pieces in information science journals on several different aspects of librarianship. His interest in journal publishing, and specifically the emerging Open Access model in the 2000s, would have been shared with many other university librarians around that time. What marked Beall out was his interest in the emails he had started to receive as a published academic author soliciting article submissions—and his decision to do something about it.

The first article Beall published on the topic was in 2009 in *The Charleston Advisor* (Beall, 2009). The article was an appraisal of Bentham Open, which had come to Beall's attention as a publisher that had started publishing over 200 journals in a relatively short period of time. Beall is scathing about the publisher's titles, awarding them just one star out of five for content, searchability, and price. In his concluding comments, he shapes some of the phrases that would become familiar to many in describing predatory journals in the future:

> Bentham Open's emergence into scholarly publishing in 2007 has served mainly as a venue to publish research of questionable quality. The site has exploited the Open Access model for its own financial motives and flooded scholarly communication with a flurry of low quality and questionable research. By linking to sites such as Bentham Open, libraries are diluting scholarly research and making it more difficult for scholars to sort through the abundance of journal articles available.
>
> (Beall, 2009)

Beall followed up this article with two more in 2010 and a fourth in 2012, which in total identified 18 publishers responsible for more than 1,300 journals (Kendall, 2021). In addition, there were another 40 or so articles that he also published up to 2018 about the dangers posed by predatory publishers, as well themes surrounding Open Access. While there are information scientists and library scholars who have published more in this period, few will have received the recognition Beall had, which included significant citation numbers accruing to his most influential articles.

According to Google Scholar, his work has received nearly 4,000 citations, with two-thirds of those occurring since 2016 when he was almost at the end of his career.

In his assessment of Beall's scholarly work, Kendall (2021) identifies three key achievements. As well as the development of the general understanding of predatory publishing, Beall created Beall's List as an important resource for researchers and in lesser-known work highlighted problems with the Impact Factor and the absence of an editor-in-chief from journals. One could add to this the highlighting of spam emails as a means of soliciting article submissions alongside other academics such as Eysenbach (2008) and Sanderson (2010). Perhaps what marked Beall out was the positive action he took against the phenomenon rather than just passively observing it from afar.

Putting aside Beall's List briefly, despite flagging the dangers of spam emails as far back as 2009, the problem seems to be more prevalent in 2021. According to Statista (2021), while spam emails decreased as a percentage of all sent emails to just less than 50 percent in 2020, they still accounted for around 150 billion emails in 2019. In their study, Wilkinson et al (2019) found that up to 10 academic spam emails (ASEs) were received by 55 percent of academics on a daily basis, with every single respondent reporting at least one received in the previous week. As well as the risk posed to academic researchers by either publishing in predatory journals or citing them, the authors also underline the time wasted in dealing with ASEs across all faculty positions.

BEALL'S LIST

What became universally known as "Beall's List" started life as a blog site called "Scholarly Open Access" in 2010 (Shamseer, 2021). Here Beall honed his identification of predatory content to the shorthand of "potential, probable or possible scholarly Open Access" and permanently included not one list but two lists: predatory journals and predatory publishers. Up until the site was taken down in early 2017, Beall posted regularly on the topic of predatory activities and Open Access journals while maintaining and growing both lists. At its peak, the lists accounted for over 1,000 individual journals and 1,000 publishers, encompassing over 7,000 journals in total (Crawford, 2017).

The establishment of Beall's List and the accompanying blog was both Beall's greatest achievement and perhaps his biggest mistake. While his early work on predatory journals and Open Access has been well cited and received, Beall's List became a focus for huge criticism despite its wide appeal among researchers the world over. The criticisms have been systematically recorded by Stephen Kimotho (Kimotho, 2021), and they can be summarized into three areas:

1. Beall's selection of both journals and publishers has been heavily criticized, both in terms of the subjectivity of any criteria used and how those criteria were applied (Shamseer, 2021). The effect was to include journals that did not seem to fit his own criteria or to include publishers where he appeared to tar all their journals with the same brush.

2. Beall also came under fire for his views on Open Access, which grew into outright criticism of the Gold OA model. In an article in 2013, he rounded on the "open-access movement" for its supposed political agenda, even accusing it of "fostering" predatory journals as a result (Beall, 2013). Unsurprisingly, this won him few friends among librarians and OA devotees.

3. While some commercial publishers may have grown to like Beall as a high-profile librarian who was anti-OA and anti-predatory publishing, some Open Access publishers included on his list were less than happy. Many publishers suffered adverse effects—and still do to this day—to the extent that one major publisher's pressure on the University of Colorado apparently hastened the shutting down of the blog site and lists.

Criticisms also centered around the unintended consequences of the negative effects of Beall's activities on both those publishers who did not regard themselves as predatory and those authors from emerging economies for whom inexpensive access to OA journals was essential

WALKING AWAY

With hindsight, it is perhaps inevitable that the criticisms he faced over Beall's List, together with the pressure of maintaining the lists while working and researching full-time, led him to shut down his website on January 15, 2017, and leave his job shortly afterward. While it seemed sudden, those who had conversations with him said that he had been contemplating such a move for some time. At the time, however, it was major news in the scholarly communications industry, with numerous stories being shared around about what had happened behind the scenes. Officially, the University of Colorado issued a statement to the website Retraction Watch to say that it was Beall's decision to step down and that it "supports and recognizes the important work Professor Beall has contributed to the field and to scholars worldwide" (retractionwatch.com, 2017). Whatever the reason, Beall's List was no more. . . . Or was it?

Almost immediately, new sites sprang up either preserving the latest version of Beall's List or pledging to maintain it to carry on Beall's work. Beallslist.net reproduced Beall's List, but also offers access to an "updated" list of publishers and journals (Beallslist.net, n.d.). A website run by an organization called "Stop Predatory Journals" (Predatoryjournals.com, n.d.) also purports to do something similar, offering lists of alleged predatory journals based on a "kernel" of information supplied by the original Beall's List. However, both these sites fail to identify who runs them or what criteria are used to maintain or update the lists of publishers and journals. Despite this, these sites and others feature highly on any search for "Beall's List" via Google and as such are likely to still be well used.

POST-BEALL ENVIRONMENT

There are legitimate concerns that lists of predatory publishers can lead to erroneous decisions by researchers on questions such as where they should publish or what research they should use or cite. And these decisions will not be improved by websites copying Beall and failing to show any transparency or evidence of their legitimacy. Other sites have been set up to provide an alternative to Beall, but some of these are also shrouded in mystery. For example, Dolos is a site developed by Professor Alexandre Georges from Toulouse University in France, but access was not possible in July 2021. In previous blog posts, Professor Georges claimed to be adding journals and magazines regularly (Researchgate.com, 2021), although the criteria he used were again unclear.

Portals have been created on a national scale as well, most notably by the Indian government under the auspices of its University Grants Commission (UGC). An initial attempt to create an approved list of journals for Indian researchers was thwarted by the inclusion of predatory journals (Patwardhan, 2019); however, a second attempt by the UGC to create a safe list of journals has now been established (UGC, 2021). In addition to specific portals, other scoring mechanisms have been suggested to help identify predatory journals. In a paper from 2013, predatory journals researcher Jaime Texeira da Silva suggested a mechanism by which journals were assigned a Predatory Score based on a complex system of quantitative measures (da Silva, 2013). While this endeavor seemed to make significant progress in framing the predatory journal problem into a more objective exercise, it did not gain much traction and to date has received 25 citations (Google Scholar, n.d.). During the mid-2010s, there seemed to be increasing awareness of the challenge posed by predatory publishing practices, but in terms of ways to tackle the issue, using Beall's List seemed to dominate people's thinking, despite numerous other attempts to mitigate the problem.

CABELLS

When Beall announced he was closing his website, one organization was more interested than perhaps any others. Since the late 1970s, Cabells—a scholarly analytics company based in Beaumont, Texas—had provided universities and other institutions a subscription service by which users could access data on academic journals to help them choose journals in which to publish. At first the company published hard copy directories focused on business and management journals—the subject area founder Dr. Dave Cabell had researched and taught in as an academic himself—before branching out into social sciences and sciences, as well as moving online. By July 2021, Cabells had indexed 11,287 journals (Cabells, n.d.), with plans to index a further 6,000 journals in the area of Medicine by the following year.

Cabells had a background, then, of evaluating journals, so in 2014 it began to investigate the idea of listing predatory journals after it had experience of predatory journals trying to infiltrate its index of recommended titles. After looking at criteria to identify predatory journals, and what made the indexed journals legitimate, it started to develop its own list. At this time, Cabells consulted with Beall himself on what to look out for, and it was at this time that Beall intimated to Cabells that he was thinking about retiring from the work he was doing on his blog in the near future. In 2015, Cabells ramped up the project, taking into account the criticism that Beall's List had received in order to establish a means of identifying and evaluating predatory journals. The criteria included some of Beall's own benchmarks, as well as those from other indexes such as Cabells' own directory (now called Journalytics), Scopus, Web of Science, and other evaluation processes. The aim, according to Cabells, was to create best practice for both identifying legitimate journals and, by contrast, highlighting those titles doing the opposite. Much of the challenge in this enterprise focused on how the rubric was implemented and where the weightings should be administered. For example, some criteria might show low-quality or niche journals as well as predatory intent, whereas others (such as lack of peer review or fallacies included on a website) were stronger indicators of predation.

In 2016, the fine-tuning of the criteria was finalized, and the focus turned to building up the database to be launched as a product in 2017. A critical mass of journals had already been evaluated by the time Beall closed his list, and product development sped up to enable Cabells to launch its Blacklist (now called *Predatory Reports*) in July 2017 with 4,000 journals included in the database.

Given the synchronicity, it has been assumed by many people in scholarly communications and academia that the Cabells database of predatory journals replaced Beall's List, took up its mantle or had acquired it. However, none of these rumors are true. While Beall was consulted in the early days of development, he never had any direct input into what Cabells was doing, and his influence was restricted to providing guidance on how to spot predatory journals. Indeed, when the database was first launched, few of the journals and publishers on Beall's List at the time of its closure were included; such was the extent to which Cabells wanted to distance themselves from the now-defunct Beall website. As of July 2021, while Cabells has an internal project to independently assess every journal and all the publishers' journals that Beall included in his list, this process has yet to be completed. As such, the overlap between Beall's List and Cabells' *Predatory Reports* database was incidental. In their analysis, Strinzel et al (2019) estimated it to be around 20 percent. Journals included by Cabells in its database tend to be suggested by users, scholarly communication professionals and those researching the area. Editors and publishers themselves often supply information as well, with increasing numbers coming from the wider academic community and through social media as general awareness of the phenomenon increases.

LEGACY

In some ways, Beall's legacy has yet to be determined, as his name and list live on in the minds of many people when they refer to predatory journals. However, we can already say with some certainty that he has had the biggest influence on the issue, both in terms of highlighting the emerging problem in the first place, and with his pro-activity in establishing Beall's List. However, it is also clear that his legacy continues to face fierce scrutiny through the criticisms of his methodology, and which journals and publishers were and were not included. The websites that purport to carry on his work do him few favors in hiding behind anonymity and opaque criteria.

Meanwhile, Beal himself has retired to the Colorado wilderness, and judging by social media concerns himself mostly with photographing stunning vistas and cataloguing some of the interesting historical and natural aspects of the state. However, there have been occasional forays into the predatory publishing debate, with salvos directed at certain journals or publishers he thinks are worthy of further investigation. Leaving behind the topic is no doubt hard to do after such immersion for many years. Especially, as we will see in the next chapter, the rise of the predatory journal was in no way halted once Beall closed his list. Quite the opposite.

CHAPTER 6

THE RISE AND RISE OF PREDATORY PRACTICES

The post-Beall era of predatory publishing practices has seen increases in the numbers of both illegitimate journals identified and investigations into their operations. One of the issues researchers faced with Beall's List was the lack of concrete data available to them to properly establish the number of predatory journals. Beall's blog page didn't identify how many journals and publishers were listed, and while the former was easy enough to count (just over 1,000 by the time Beall's List was discontinued in early 2017), it was not known how many journals the 1,000 or so publishers listed were responsible for. The introduction of Cabells' *Journal Blacklist* in July 2017 for the first time introduced verifiable data that provided a clearer picture.

That said, some academics had attempted to provide more detail, most notably Shen and Björk (2015), which as we shall see in this chapter enabled other researchers and scholars in general to appreciate for perhaps the first time what the scale of the predatory problem might be. This was especially true of the impact predatory journals were having on certain countries, with some experiencing greater problems than others, or seeing problems where it was assumed they didn't exist. The post-Beall era saw the wider impact of predatory practices more generally take hold, with predatory conferences, books and repositories being widely reported on. Knock-on effects also started to make themselves felt, such as the implications for research funders and universities once it became known their money had supported predatory publications and conference attendance. In the immediate aftermath of Beall's List, predatory practices became an even hotter topic than it had been before.

THE WORLD'S PROBLEM

In 2015 an article entitled " 'Predatory Open Access': a longitudinal study of article volumes and market characteristics" by Cenyu Shen and Bo-Christer Björk appeared in the journal *BMC Medicine*—it went on to become one of the seminal articles of the nascent predatory publishing research area. From its publication in 2015 until August 2021, it has been cited 645 times according to Google Scholar, making it one of the most cited articles on the topic of predatory publishing. For many people, the results of the study would have come as a huge shock, as it was one of the first attempts to estimate the scale of the predatory publishing problem. Shen and Björk put the number of predatory journals at around 8,000 in 2014, publishing 420,000 articles in total (Shen and Björk, 2015).

The authors also shone a spotlight on where predatory journals and the authors publishing in them were based, identifying over a quarter of all predatory publishers and over a third of all authors as being based in India, with Asia, Africa, and North America also figuring prominently (Shen and Björk, 2015). Again, it was the first time that many people would have understood the global nature of the problem, as well as connecting the spam emails that blighted many academics' email inboxes with a widespread publishing phenomenon.

As with Beall, the importance of the Shen and Björk article is substantial but not without controversy. As with many of the articles published in the early and mid-2010s, the authors used Beall's List journals and publishers as their data source. However, as we have seen in the previous chapter, there are many problems with the verifiability of Beall's data, and therefore any study that uses that data will also face the same criticism. In addition, some critics have pointed to the headline number of 420,000 articles as simply unrealistic. As Teixeira de Silva points out, the extrapolation from shaky foundations in the shape of Beall's List means that the study's results have to be questioned (Teixeira de Silva, 2017).

PREDATOR EFFECT

The question marks around Beall's List, Shen and Björk's article and other studies in the mid-2010s, however, fail to mask the growing, multi-faceted problems predatory practices had introduced to scholarly communications. In several ways, these impacts were beginning to become clearer, and were starting to alarm scholars, publishers and universities alike. These impacts can be summarized as deleterious effects on national research programs, subject disciplines, and research funding.

Since 2018, several articles and reports have been published identifying problems resulting from predatory publishing activities in various countries. Perhaps the hardest hitting of these was the investigation undertaken by a collaboration of journalists in Germany, which sought to shine a light on the many shady publications and outcomes involving German academics and organizations (Krause and Langhans, 2018). For example, they found that 5,000 individual authors from Germany had published in predatory journals in recent years, and that employees from 12 of the 30 DAX-listed companies had articles published. The seedy nature of the predatory publishing enterprise, and the fact that German research was being shared without proper peer review checks, caused a major stir in a country that has seen numerous academic scandals in recent times with ministers forced to resign over plagiarism allegations.

Other countries to see their involvement highlighted in academic investigations include Russia (Abalkina, 2021), Nordic states (Bjork, 2019), South Korea (Park et al, 2019), and Uzbekistan (Eschanov et al, 2019). Several articles have taken a wider view to highlight that certain countries are impacted to a greater extent—in terms of both the numbers of authors who publish in predatory journals and the number of journals that appear to be based in specific countries (Shen and Bjork, 2015).

When specific subject disciplines are considered, the effect seems to be more concentrated on STEM subjects, with medical topics in particular spawning thousands of fake journals. According to Cabells data, over 4,300 journals claim to publish articles in the medical field (this includes multidisciplinary journals), or around a third of the journals in its *Predatory Reports* database (Linacre, 2020c). Within medicine, numerous articles have appeared warning researchers of the emergence of predatory journals, such as in pathology (Vranic et al, 2018) or dentistry (Keough, 2020). However, other disciplines have also seen the predator effect manifest itself, such as economics (Tarejo-Pech et al, 2021). What is interesting is that while each discipline suffers from exposure to predatory journals, the investigations referenced here each identify effects that seem to be specific to the subject areas involved.

Finally, underpinning publications and research is the matter of funding, and the extent to which funders are aware of the predatory publishing phenomenon. We will see in the next section just how much money from funding may find its way into predatory publishers' pockets, but it is a statement of fact that predatory journals rely on authors paying APCs to ensure publication of their article, and the capital required for that payment will often come from their research grant, whether it be internally from their institution or externally from a third-party funder. Shamseer (2021) identified 236 biomedical predatory journals publishing 3,702 articles, with 1,907 of those featuring either primary research or systematic reviews of humans or animals. Those 1,907 articles were then assessed for support from funders. In total, there were 345 acknowledgments of funding in 323 articles, with the National Institutes of Health (NIH) being the most common funder with 41 instances, followed by Indian funders the Universities Grants Commission (15) and the Indian Council of Medical Research (8). As Shamseer notes, the implication is that millions of animals and thousands of humans have been involved in experiments that have led to publications with little or no peer review, and a substantial waste of both funding resources and scientific endeavor, as the articles are often weak and won't receive the usage or citations that articles in reputable journals will gain.

LEAKAGE AND CONTAMINATION

The two main impacts of predatory journals center around the waste of university and third-party funding resources, as well as the contamination of the academic record as articles are read, cited and used by academics and society in general. In 2018, the Federal Trade Commission (FTC) concluded its investigation of perhaps the best known and biggest predatory publisher, OMICS International (OMICS). After looking into its activities over a six-year period during the 2010s, it found that OMICS had effectively defrauded the authors paying to publish OA articles in its journals, issuing a fine of $50.1 million (FTC, 2019). The judgment was significant for several reasons, not least that the FTC laid down a precedent for what services authors could expect from an academic journal, and it put a figure on how much predatory publishing might be worth.

Extrapolating this data, Linacre (2020b) estimated that the predatory journal market could be worth at least $75–$100 million a year. In other words, authors and funders are losing this amount every year to nefarious operators, with little or no return on their investment as articles tend not to be used or cited by others. When a figure like this is provided, it is possible to see the damage predatory journals can have as a consequence of the exploitation of scholarly communications.

If one consequence is a leakage of funding, a second result of this activity is the contamination of other legitimate academic publications. This can come in several different guises. For example, an author may read an article published in an academic journal and believe that its findings have been peer reviewed and include it as support for their own research. However, this article will likely not have been peer reviewed, and as such may be completely bogus or make fundamental errors. This illegitimate research then contaminates otherwise good research, bringing into question the legitimacy of the second article. It is difficult to determine the extent of this contamination. If we take as an example the first OMICS journal listed alphabetically in the Cabells *Predatory Reports* database—*Abnormal and Behavioural Psychology*—and use citation software Publish or Perish (https://harzing.com/blog/2021/10/publish-or-perish, Version 7) to analyze the journal's citation activity, we see that in the three-year period 2015–2017 it had nine articles (out of a total of 27 published) cited a total of 44 times. This random example shows that while predatory journal articles don't have the status of more reputable journals, nor do they go unnoticed in the academic record.

This record does not simply include the articles themselves, however. So-called ghost journals are titles that have been indexed and subsequently removed but whose data may still be included in the index. A study by Cortegiani et al into Scopus and DOAJ found that while journals had been removed from databases due to concerns of their publishing practices, they had continued to be cited, many at a higher rate than when they were included (Cortegiani et al, 2020).

DAMAGE LIMITATION

Other negative consequences of predatory journals include offshoots such as predatory conferences and author services, as well as links to other nefarious practices in scholarly communications such as paper mills. In his piece for the Scholarly Kitchen blog in 2018, Crotty pointed to numerous posts the blog had included over a six-year period on the topic of predatory journals, which included impacts such as the negative perception it had given legitimate OA journals, a breakdown of trust in general with academic publishing, and an overview of what can happen to authors who publish articles in predatory journals in good faith (Crotty, 2018).

Other negative impacts can revolve around unintended consequences, such as authors who submit and publish to predatory journals that have similar names to other, more reputable journals (Likis, 2019). The impact has even been felt by authors who have not published in predatory journals, as almost any academic with a publishing record will find themselves "spammed" by predatory journals soliciting content. It has been estimated that this email torrent costs up to $1.1 billion a year, in addition to the time wasted by academics dealing with the problem (Linacre, 2020a).

Bringing the growth in predatory journals up to the present day, the problem appears to be as prevalent as ever:

- As of May 8, 2022, Cabells listed 16,169 journals in its *Predatory Reports* database, adding around 150 journals a month for the previous three years (Linacre, 2021b)
- New strategies are emerging, such as "retconning" and bootlegging. Retconning refers to the rebranding of identified predatory journals under new titles or publisher brands, while bootlegging practices include the plagiarizing and appropriating of articles already published in legitimate journals and passing them off as original works (Siler et al, 2021; Amrit, 2021)
- Early data from a new service offered by author services firm Inera through its Edifix product, which allows authors to check the references from their articles with journals listed by Cabells, showed that 4 percent of article references checked were from predatory journals,

with 22 percent of the articles including multiple predatory references (Linacre, 2021a)

- A survey conducted by the InterAcademy Partnership (IAP) showed that almost a quarter of academics surveyed had either published in a predatory journal, contributed to a predatory conference, or did not know if they had (IAP, 2022).

This small but significant activity backs up other recent research (Schira and Hurst, 2019; Collom et al, 2020), and begs the question as to whether authors can do more to prevent falling into the traps being laid for them by predatory publishers. The IAP survey also asked academics what they thought would happen if predatory publishing practices were left unchallenged, and 82 percent said it would fuel misinformation in public policy, with 58 percent thinking it would widen the research gap between high income and low-income countries—another unintended consequence of predatory journals. It seems that authors have the will to provide solutions, and yet are also directly involved in the problem.

ENHANCED ROLE OF THE LIBRARIAN

Such an assessment may appear a little bleak, and the publication of the IAP report (2022) has not only shone further light on the problem of predatory publishing, but also provided numerous solutions as a result of its wide-ranging engagement with key stakeholders such as publishers, funders and librarians. Indeed, academic librarians as a group perhaps offer one of the keys to unlocking the problem of predatory journals given their role, knowledge and extended remit when it comes to advising authors on publishing decisions.

First, librarians have traditionally been the architects of the holdings universities have had to supply their academic researchers and students with the resources they need. This role, however, has changed with Open Access content as the control librarians could have over what resources are used has diminished. But for many librarians, this has been an opportunity to expand their role into advising their academic colleagues where and how to publish and bring their formidable knowledge of the academic publishing landscape to bear. Certainly, any university that has fostered this type of role for its librarians will be reducing the chances of its researchers making unwise publishing decisions.

And secondly, many librarians have played an active role in highlighting the problems of predatory journals, impacting discussions and raising the profile of the debate in author and publishing communities. In addition to the huge part played by Beall that we saw in the previous chapter, notable commentators such as Lisa Hinchliffe (2019) and Ruth Pagell (2019) have shown leadership in their knowledge sharing and insight into the predatory publishing problem. While authors may find themselves in an invidious position when it comes to the threat they face with the rise and impact of predatory journals, at least in librarians they have someone both knowledgeable and trustworthy to support them.

CHAPTER 7

UNAWARE OR UNETHICAL?
AUTHOR MOTIVATIONS

One of the criticisms leveled at those who research and comment on predatory publishing is that it is simply an unknown quantity. As we saw in Chapter 2, defining predatory publishing has proven difficult, and the definition adopted for this book does lack a little sharpness by necessity, with too little clarity about several of the murkier aspects of the phenomenon. However, as we have seen through examinations of journal development, Open Access models, and predatory journal lists, these journals are very much in existence and should be taken with due seriousness by authors.

In parallel to the somewhat ethereal nature of predatory journals and the extent to which there is an intention to deceive on behalf of the publisher, there is the often-unknown quantity of the author who publishes in such journals, specifically centering around their motivation. If we take at face value Shen and Bjork's (2015) estimate of 420,000 article publications in predatory journals annually, that will mean hundreds of thousands of authors having submitted and paid for journals in fake journals. Did they do so unwittingly, or did publication serve as a convenient means to an end?

CAVEAT SCRIPTOR

The problems facing authors with regard to predatory journals can be summed up with the plight of an academic this author met in Kuwait in the mid-2010s. Under pressure from his institution to publish in English-language journals, he submitted, paid for, and published an article in a journal that he subsequently discovered to be predatory. In panic, he asked his superior what he should do, and the sympathetic senior academic advised he should publish the article again in a different, more reputable journal. Not understanding the problems associated with dual publication, he duly submitted the article again, which was published by the second journal. Problem solved, or so he thought, until a certain publishing executive gave a presentation at his institution and described the breach of publication ethics surrounding the submission of the same article to two different journals.

The moral of this story? Well, for one, authors should be very much aware of all aspects of publication ethics, which, despite their importance and career-threatening consequences, are rarely taught in any depth at even the most research-intensive universities. However, even if adequate training were given to all postgraduates as potential authors, many would still fall for predatory scams and may even be alerted to the attractiveness of guaranteed publication in a matter of days for just a few hundred dollars.

Sadly, there has been little research done in this area so far, presumably because those authors who have published in predatory journals would rather not acknowledge and answer any questions about it. In the next section, we will look in depth at one of the few published articles focused explicitly on author motivations, which centers on whether authors are either unaware they have published in fake journals or are fully aware and have few qualms about doing so.

UNAWARE OR UNETHICAL . . . OR BOTH?

The standout research in the area of author motivations relating to predatory journals was published in 2017 by Denmark-based academic Tove Faber Frandsen (Frandsen, 2017). The central question of "unaware or unethical" in the heading of this chapter summarizes the key finding in Frandsen's article, which had two main research questions:

1. Are authors citing potential predatory journals and potential poor scientific standards journals predominantly from developing countries?
2. Are authors citing potential predatory journals and potential poor scientific standards journals generally inexperienced authors with few publications and citations?

In the article, Frandsen addressed a few assumptions in academia and scholarly publishing about who these authors were who actually published in predatory journals. These assumptions range from those who think that nobody could be so naïve as to publish in such journals to those who believe nobody in the West would stoop so low as to publish in such journals. There are a whole range of prejudices to unpack in these and other thoughts around the motivations behind authors publishing in predatory journals, which is the context around the research conducted by Frandsen.

The study first looks at the literature on author motivations to publish in predatory journals, which is limited to say the least. Authors have not typically come forward when prompted about publishing in such journals, and Frandsen references the German study we saw in Chapter 6 where not one of the 5,000 German authors identified as having published in predatory journals came forward (Krause and Langhans, 2018). What few studies exist show that the reasons authors cite for publishing in predatory journals come down to awareness (or lack thereof) or motivation. The latter is interesting, as this covers different motivations such as the perceived ease with which publications can lead to promotion or a cynical dissatisfaction with the scholarly communications industry as a whole (Frandsen, 2017).

Frandsen also offers some solutions, based around the education of authors on the inherent issues associated with predatory journals, but also with a review of how incentives and rewards can lead to authors being tempted to make the wrong choices. It is worth reminding ourselves why authors want to publish in the first place at this point, and typically it is for one or more of four reasons: to register an idea or experiment or finding; to certify and validate research; to disseminate that research; and to archive the research for future reference. Frandsen's study is backed up by Yeoh et al (2017), who found similar motivations and called for a new tranche of legitimate publishing outlets to support academics from developing countries to present their research in a safe environment away from the reach of predatory journals.

It is perhaps instructive to review these traditional motivations through the lens of predatory publishing, where authors might be led to believe they are achieving all these outcomes but in fact can fail at each one. In turn, they may register their idea, but do so in the wrong place without any prospect of changing; any certification is superficial without proper peer review;

dissemination is very poor in predatory journals and sometimes nonexistent; and there are few if any guarantees of secure archiving as the thousands of empty journals that exist attest.

PUSHMI-PULLYU

So, is Frandsen right in saying that it is broadly a combination of unethical and unaware authors who contribute to predatory journals? While there are few other articles directly answering the question of author motivation, there is a healthy volume of papers that look at why authors might be tempted. These come in two forms, essentially dependent on push or pull factors. On the push side, the well-known "publish or perish" phenomenon is quoted extensively, describing cultures in higher education where there is both the implicit and explicit encouragement for academics to publish their research, often following fairly prescriptive lists of the "right" journals. Incentives have come in the shape of financial awards in countries like China or research grants in Australia for publishing in top-ranked journals, and on the flip side elsewhere a lack of promotion opportunities or even the sack if publishing targets aren't met.

For an insight into the quandaries often faced by authors, one need only look to India, where the numbers of authors publishing in predatory journals and the number of journals themselves are perhaps the largest in the world (Shen and Bjork, 2015). In an article investigating the problem, a call was made for the Indian government to step in (Seethapathy et al, 2016), and in the years following, numerous attempts were made by the UGC to create lists of both preferred and questionable journals for Indian authors to publish in. In the original investigation, authors found to have published in a sample of Beall's List journals cited help with promotion and institutional pressures as the two greatest push factors—although it is also worth noting that a majority also denied that the journals they had published in were predatory.

This brings into focus the difficulties felt by two communities of authors in particular—early career scholars (ECRs) and those from the Global South. As Nicholas et al pointed out in their study of ECRs (2020), there is considerable concern among them about predatory journals, with 10 percent saying they avoided publishing in OA journals because of the perceived poor quality of them, in part due to the predatory publishing phenomenon. Perhaps just as revealingly, the first two reasons given by ECRs for not publishing in OA journals—prohibitive costs (38%) and lack of available options (21%)—are two of the key selling points predatory publishers use to lure authors into publishing with them. These concerns are likely to be particularly acute for ECRs based at universities in the Global South where there is likely to be less financial support for paying high OA fees or a support structure designed to help them make informed decisions about publication outlets. However, it is important to point out that while many countries in the Global South figured among the top countries for authors who have published in predatory journals in Shen and Bjork's study, countries outside, such as the United States, were also prominent, so it is too simplistic to suggest that predatory journals are "just" a problem for those countries.

Other problems emanating from initial push factors include asymmetries of information. For example, where predatory journals have found themselves included in databases used for publication recommendation, this can attract other submissions. In Italy, this was found to be the case in a large survey of Italian authors, in addition to a "hedging your bets"–type strategy where a push for authors to publish in journals was not regulated by publishing experts (Bagues et al, 2017).

Strong pressure to publish in certain journals can undoubtedly produce the right circumstances for gaming to occur, and publishing mandates may also stimulate this behavior. This is a concern held by some around OA mandates, as they could persuade authors to publish in cheap and quick predatory journals to tick the right OA box (Linacre et al, 2019). However, while the potential is there for OA mandates to add to the problem of predatory publishing behaviors, there is no evidence to suggest this is happening, with some studies suggesting that from an OA perspective the number of articles being included in predatory journals may be decreasing (Eykens et al, 2019).

When we look at the consequences of pull factors in academia related to predatory journals, we can see the temptations that lure authors, such as promises of fast publication times from the frequent email invitations academics tend to receive on a regular basis. Speed to publication is often top of the publishing wish list for authors, and knowing that an article will be published quickly may incentivize authors submitting to predatory journals, which often lead with promises of fast turnaround times (Linacre et al, 2019). Such author decisions may be triggered by emails that promise fast publishing times as well as other simply too-good-to-be-true offers that aim to stimulate the desired response in authors. In one study, of the few authors who responded to a survey on publishing in questionable journals, over two-fifths said they initially identified the journal they submitted to from soliciting emails (Cobey et al, 2017b).

Simple convenience may also be a pull factor, which the controversial Thompson Rivers University (TRU) scandal in Canada perhaps demonstrates. In 2017, TRU academic Derek Pyne published a paper investigating the publishing habits of some of his colleagues and other academics, claiming that publications in questionable journals were for some researchers correlated with receiving internal research awards (Pyne, 2017). While some of this research has been questioned (Tsigaris and Teixeira da Silva, 2019), the underlying point still holds that pull factors linked to predatory journals have the potential to influence the decision-making of academic researchers.

Aside from the motivations reported by Frandsen, Demir has also studied why authors published in predatory journals and put forward some other explanations (2018). Demir suggests that some authors, having been unsuccessful in submitting their journals to legitimate, indexed journals, decided to publish in predatory journals to ensure their work would not be lost and at least be part of the scholarly record somewhere. In addition, Demir reports that some authors may realize how difficult it is for them to publish in indexed journals, so they choose the predatory journal route. Interestingly, Demir believes that most authors choose predatory journals knowingly, with few being unaware as argued in other studies.

POSSIBLE SOLUTIONS

Whatever the route taken by authors into the pages of predatory journals, it is worth underlining that the impact can be substantial. Elsewhere in this book we have seen that research on Covid, pharmaceuticals, or engineering have the potential to leak out and contaminate the scholarly record, and as predatory journals tend to be OA in nature, that contamination can spread into the public consciousness. And while push and pull factors play a major part in this, it should also be reaffirmed that an adherence to publication ethics guidelines would mitigate many of these problems in the first place.

This is the conclusion reached by Masic in their revealing editorial piece on being invited to serve as an editor-in-chief on a *Forensic Anthropology* journal published by OMICS. After falling for the initial approach to edit a new journal as it was in their scope of interest, they were recruited to supply editorial board members, only for them to be cut off and ignored once the board members' details had been shared. Despite numerous attempts, Masic received no reply from OMICS, which in the meantime used his name and that of his contacts to promote and solicit manuscripts from authors to be published in the journal. Masic's entreaty at the end of the article is for authors to take responsibility in checking for publisher and journal reliability, publications ethics, and peer review standards.

However, such actions would always be voluntary, so other solutions that can help form a safety net for authors will always be welcome. Aside from more effective education packages for researchers, other recommendations have included open peer review so that author and peer reviewer can be held accountable (Dobusch and Heimstädt, 2019) or even holding predatory journal publication as an act of misconduct in that it evidences a willful avoidance of peer review (Yeo-Teh and Tang, 2021). Perhaps what is also needed is third-party help to support the academic author to succeed in publishing their research, and it is this help that we will be looking at in depth in the next chapter.

CHAPTER 8

FIGHTING BACK AGAINST
THE PREDATOR

A report published in 2021 by the International Science Council entitled "Opening the Record of Science: Making Scholarly Publishing Work for Science in the Digital Era" (ISC, 2021) recognized that predatory publishing was one of the challenges facing scientific endeavor in the digital space, concluding the following about predatory journals:

> The harm that such journals do is to use up the time and resources of academics who might otherwise be better employed, and to contribute to the long tail of inconsequential research. An important priority therefore is to find ways in which such actions are not incentivized, and that potential authors and readers are directed away from such journals.
>
> (ISC, 2021; P. 34)

The report neatly contextualizes the problems researchers face—and scholarly communications in particular—regarding predatory journals, mirroring much of what has been covered in the book. While it falls short of providing any answers, it does at least identify the two broad areas where solutions to the predatory problem might be found, namely in changes to the structures of incentives offered to academics for publishing their research and strategies that mitigate against authors' engagement with predatory journals. In this chapter, we will review how authors have been guided regarding the threat of predatory journals and how this guidance varied depending on regions and institutions and offer a grounded way forward for all authors based around the twin pillars of structures and strategies.

TRIED AND TESTED?

Ever since Beall and others started identifying predatory journals in the late 2000s, librarians, legitimate publishers, and university administrators have been warning authors against publishing in predatory journals. Indeed, why else would the process of identification have started in the first place other than to express concern that authors could be hoodwinked if they were not aware of the emerging problems of predatory journals. However, at the very least the jury is out as to whether such warnings were sufficiently heeded, given the growth in predatory publishing and related activities over the following decade or so.

Whatever the rights or wrongs of those early authors who identified predatory journals and the problems they posed for scholarly communications, they did the whole of science a huge favor in highlighting the issue for everyone to see. However, part of the ensuing problem of predation was that not everyone did see this early work. Beall and others tended to publish in journals focused on librarianship, information studies, or more generic journals that did not have great reach among researchers in general. Indeed, a cursory look at the bibliography of this book shows relatively few articles on predatory publishing in mainstream journals such as *Nature* or *Science*, with many articles published either in discipline-specific titles or relatively niche periodicals.

As a result, it is fair to assume that many researchers remained unaware of predatory journals until articles such as those by Josh Bohannon hit the mainstream, where predatory practices were highlighted following sting operations with nonsense or illogical articles accepted by questionable journals (Bohannon, 2013). Bohannon's article—which has become so famous it even has its own Wikipedia page (Wikipedia, 2021b)—genuinely brought predatory publishing's nefarious practices to the forefront of scientific discussions, as well as highlighting some weak processes on other more supposedly legitimate journals. Since then, however, despite a spike in interest in the phenomenon and development of a sub-discipline of research in its own right, authors from all around the globe are still publishing in predatory journals. While some of the journals listed on Cabells' *Predatory Reports* are empty or defunct, the fact that around 150 live journals were being added each month in 2021 (Linacre, 2021b) suggests that there is still demand out there, whatever is driving that demand.

CODES OF CONDUCT?

If we break down the ways of combating predatory journals into structures and strategies, the first of these themes can then be further broken down into two broad areas: categorization and Open Access. Categorization has traditionally been a key part of a librarian's role in a university, encompassing subscriptions to collections as well as recommending Open Access resources. Of course, monitoring access to OA journals is much more difficult when it does not go through an institution's subscription systems, but categorization is also done at a much wider level through indexes such as Web of Science, Scopus, DOAJ, or Cabells' Journalytics database, so-called abstracting and indexing services (A&I), which tend to focus on certain subject areas, or, widest of all, the International Standard Serial Number, aka ISSN.

Predatory journals, however, also cause problems for indices and ISSN itself. Indices and A&I services are constantly on the lookout for predatory journals, but they have nevertheless found themselves included in some of them. In addition, a tactic used by predatory publishers to add the veneer of legitimacy to their journal homepages is to add a list of indices and their logos to them. These are often fake (e.g. claiming a journal has an Impact Factor when it does not), trivial (e.g. claiming Google Scholar has indexed a journal—anyone may find the journal via Google Scholar, but that does not equate to indexing), or invented (e.g. there are many indices that are only found on predatory journal homepages and links either lead nowhere or to a basic website with few index-related details).

As for ISSN, this is another adoption made by predatory journals to lend them credibility; however, ISSN merely checks journals for evidence of publication and not for their legitimacy as journals. In 2020, 40 percent of titles listed on Cabells' *Predatory Reports* had ISSN codes (Linacre, 2020d) with 90 percent of those journals being added in June 2021 also including the code (Linacre, 2021c). Moreover, many of those journals that publish an ISSN have made the code up or copied it from a legitimate journal. Therefore, despite complex and multi-layered categorization existing in scholarly communication, it has little effect on halting the operations of predatory publishers.

ROLE OF OPEN ACCESS

The second strand of the structural piece is the role OA plays in terms of how predatory journals have developed and continue to thrive. We saw in the discussion of Beall that he seemed to lay a lot of responsibility at the door of OA for the growth of predatory journals, and he was heavily criticized for this stance among OA advocates. While OA offers the opportunity for bad actors to take advantage of a business model that includes authors paying fees to be published, this is by no means the ONLY way to ensure OA publication. Many journals listed on DOAJ have no fees for authors whatsoever, while preprints— or "Green OA"—offer authors an opportunity to make their research openly available outside journals and without APCs. Could, therefore, OA itself offer a solution to the predatory journal problem?

The Covid-19 pandemic has seen a greater focus on preprints, and thousands of articles have been posted to repositories—or preprint servers—to enable the research to be released more quickly, circumventing the often time-intensive peer review process. However, this has also highlighted an innate concern with Green OA channels in that there is usually no peer review, and therefore poor or junk science can reach a wide audience. Articles promoting the use of Hydroxychloroquine or Invermectin have found their way into mainstream social media from repositories and predatory journals, despite the fact there is no serious support for their effectiveness (Rhode and Linacre, n.d.).

Others have recommended wholesale changes to OA and scholarly communications to create a new framework that, if implemented, would mitigate against predatory journals having a wider impact. Green (2019) argues that accepting preprints into what he refers to as the "reputation economy" is the only way to progress fully with OA principles while taking advantage of increasingly digital workflows for authors, universities, and publishers alike.

This would not see the end of journals; rather, it would introduce a market where all articles are "born OA" in repositories and then developed, reviewed, and published subsequently by journals. This, of course, already happens for many articles, but Green suggests the whole of academic publishing should work within this framework. More pertinent to our subject, perhaps, is Green's further claim that by improving the acceptability of preprints, authors would be less inclined to seek publication and therefore demand for predatory journals would decrease. The logic here certainly makes sense as we have seen how the need to publish drives many authors' motivations for publishing in predatory journals. However, what is still unclear is how quickly the culture of academia would change so that authors were not bothered about publishing in journals, if it would change at all.

STRATEGIC FOCUS

Moving on to the second way of combating predatory publishing activities, several different strategies have been suggested over the last decade or so to fight back and even overwhelm fake journals. When one talks to publishers or academics, almost everyone has their own pet theory about how to defeat predatory journals, and here is just a selection of strategies and research articles suggesting different strategic approaches:

- Avoid them: by identifying them using warning lists such as *Predatory Reports* or strategies using websites such as Think. Check. Submit
- Raise awareness: by introducing education and training programs, or by improving understanding of the nature of research and the context it is published in (Rice et al, 2021)
- Intervene: by governmental agencies to identify and take down predatory journal sites (IAP, 2021)
- Wicked problem: understand the problem as a complex, nonhomogeneous entity and act according to circumstances (Kratochvil et al, 2020)
- Laissez-faire approach: simply don't worry about the problem and understand predatory journals are a relatively low-priority consequence of the wider benefits of an open access model (Brembs, 2015) with little scientific impact (Bjork et al, 2019).

Further to these specific strategies, another tactic employed by many editors and authors in medical journals has been to write editorials in journals warning their communities about predatory journals and suggesting researchers "fight back" against the problem. For example, Mathew et al (2021) wrote in Current Problems in Diagnostic Radiology that "the authenticity and confidence of scientific work from around the world has been systemically corrupted by predatory journals" and warned readers of the implications to patient care and research if the phenomenon remained unchecked. Often scholars are asked to help by conducting further research by those writing about predatory journals or publication ethics more widely, and there are numerous continuing research projects in 2021 based at Texas Tech University, the University of Ottowa, and by IAP to name just a few.

More rarely—but perhaps more interestingly—some scholars have used their research to go further than merely report their findings with regard to predatory publishing and use their research as a platform to recommend systemic changes or broader strategies to deal with the problem. Da Silva et al (2021) found that identifying predatory journals was inevitably difficult as journals inhabited a spectrum of quality and deception. As such, the authors recommended a credit rating-style system that scores journals according to their scholarliness (or lack of) to be used with existing safe lists and their criteria.

Going one step further, Shamseer (2021) has published an entire Ph.D. thesis about predatory publishing, with much of the document proposing a variety of solutions in addition to a comprehensive academic deep dive into the subject. Suggestions for mitigating the problems caused by predatory journals include better understanding of the wasted academic research lost in predatory journals (i.e. research leakage) and an enhanced role for funders to play in both knowing where their monies are being employed and when they have been done so irresponsibly to pay for APCs and publications in predatory journals.

PRACTICAL STEPS

Whatever the good intentions of the scholars and organizations noted earlier, despite the structures and strategies that are in place or that have been argued for, authors in their thousands have published and continue to publish in predatory journals. So, what should they do if the worst has happened? To end this chapter—and as a segue into the final chapter where we will look at recent innovations and try to gaze a little into the future—here are five handy tips in the style of a Q&A for authors concerned about predatory publications based on some research (Linacre, 2021d) and prior experience of the author:

Q. How can you detect and avoid predatory journals?

Research the topic and use the many guidelines provided by university libraries around the world. You can also use Cabells' own criteria that it uses to identify predatory journals for inclusion in its Predatory Reports database.

Q. What is the warning sign that a journal or publisher is predatory?

In addition to the common indicators listed here, other more superficial signs can include poor grammar/spelling, very broad coverage of a topic, or solicitation of article submissions with excessive flattery in spam emails.

Q. What steps can I take to minimize the chance of publishing in a predatory journal?

There are three things every author can do to mitigate the chances of publishing in the wrong journals: check your choices of journal with trusted colleagues, librarians, and senior academics; ensure all details shared about the journal such as publisher location, editor affiliation, and citation database claims check out; and confirm that the journal is included in multiple, respected journal databases such as Scopus, Web of Science, Cabells' Journalytics, or DOAJ.

Q. What happens if you publish in a predatory journal?

It stays published—retraction is highly unlikely, and to try and republish the article in a legitimate journal will only compound the problem by breaching publication ethics guidelines.

Q. What should you do if you realize you have published in a predatory journal?

Inform any co-authors, your institution, and any funders that have supported your research, and be honest about the mistake. Your institution may also be able to help you to try and obtain a retraction.

Q. Does it mean my research is lost if I have published in a predatory journal?

No. You can try to develop the published research in a different direction and write an entirely new article and try to get it published in a legitimate journal, explaining to relevant editors a previous article was published in a predatory journal.

CHAPTER 9
A DIGITAL FUTURE

When publishing started to go online in the 1990s, many publishers and research integrity professionals thought that the advent of the internet and tools to search it effectively would lead to the eradication of issues such as plagiarism and dual publication. These transgressions of publishing ethics often went undetected, and indeed examples of plagiarized articles still crop up to shame academics or members of governments. It was felt that the increased threat of being caught would deter any would-be transgressors.

However, in a parallel to the advent of predatory publishing, problems with plagiarism seemed to get worse and persist to this day despite sophisticated checking tools such as iThenticate (www.ithenticate.com/). The problem for those who thought things would improve is that, as with predatory publishing activities, the internet makes the act of plagiarizing so much easier in the first place, enabling people to copy and paste from the most obscure of sources and slicing multiple sources up to evade detection. What the digital hand seemed to give to the scholarly communications industry, it also seemed to take away.

Predatory publishers have exploited digital communications for commercial gain—that much should be clear from the story that has been told in this book. But to end on what could be a positive note, this final chapter will look at the emerging digital technologies that are leading the fight back against predatory publishing practices and assess which tools and strategies may be the most effective. In summarizing the establishment, growth, and fight back against predatory journals, answers will also be suggested to some of the main outstanding questions raised in the book.

NEW DEVELOPMENTS

While digital innovation has fueled predatory practices, it can also enable technical solutions. One such solution currently under development is to use software embedded in firewalls to alert institutional users of any websites they visit that publish predatory content and any spam email they may receive is related to similar sources. If made available, this could reduce the huge amount of aggregated time and resources spent by researchers on dealing with deceptive journals.

Funders have also been encouraged to do more to mitigate against the risk of the recipients spending some of their grants on predatory journal APCs. In her PhD thesis, Shamseer (2021) is particularly vocal in her support of such moves, advocating that health funders should provide more guidance to grant recipients on how to choose suitable journals to publish their findings and ensure it is discoverable by the general public. Shamseer used to be based at the Centre for Journalology at the The Ottawa Hospital Research Institute, which has proposed developing a "Journal Authenticator Tool" as part of a number of tactics to reduce the impact of predatory journals. The Tool would "provide information about a given journal's operations and transparency practices" (ohri.com, 2021), enabling users to become more informed about the journal's practices and whether to use it for whatever purpose. This would require development using APIs to implement the tool.

In the previous chapter we also saw some suggestions based around technology to enable research communities to "fight back" against the predatory threat, such as credit-style ratings or enhanced preprint server functionality. But perhaps the most technologically advanced solution combats not just predatory journals but the problem of contamination we saw earlier. A software solution from technology services firm Inera allows authors to run a check of their references, including against the *Predatory Reports* database maintained by Cabells (https://edifix.com/). This check therefore allows authors to prevent references from predatory journals to leak into not only their own research but also anyone else's who in the future wanted to use their work. In 2021 this solution was just in a pilot phase, but it was initially reported that 4 percent of checks included at least one reference from a journal included in Cabells' *Predatory Reports* database (Linacre, 2021a). Using technology to improve hygiene factors such as legitimate references may be another strategy that, if adopted together and more widely, will have a significant impact on predatory journal output.

Further, checking software has also been reported in the academic literature, such as PedCheck (Dadkhah et al, 2022), which is a tool that has been created to identify what authors have shared about predatory journals on social media with a view to providing a wider understanding of how such journals are concerning academic researchers and which ones are particularly active.

ARTIFICIAL INTELLIGENCE

As with many problems, some people think that artificial intelligence (AI) could help with predatory publishing problems and in some way run checks against journals to ensure they are legitimate. However, such a solution has yet to emerge, and any that do will probably require either key agencies—such as editorial management software companies—or individuals to feed into a central database of information. However, competing interests may mean this could prove difficult.

In the absence of any silver bullet from technology, there are some ideas that have been put forward that at least in theory could provide some efficacy in tackling the problem. West and Bergstrom (2021) look at the problem in terms of misinformation and as such suggest a coordinated approach on behalf of policy makers and funders alike to support public outreach initiatives that promote media literacy, data reasoning, and philosophy of science. The authors, by drawing larger parallels with misinformation and issues such as fake news, highlight the core concern about public trust. If trust is lost in academic research as a result of predatory publishing activities, then the consequences could be severe.

However, the risk with any idea, technology, or initiative that seeks to eradicate predatory behavior is that it has minimal impact as the protagonists see the threat to their business model and pivot accordingly. An example of this has occurred during the Covid-19 pandemic. The sudden lockdown and near eradication of in-person conferences during 2020 and into 2021 would have obviously had an impact on predatory conference organizers, who would be unable to persist with their scams without any academic posteriors on their conference seats. However, like mainstream conferences, predatory events were able to move online and even exploit a different business model (Lenhart, 2021). Instead of charging a few hundred dollars for attendance, they were able to recruit plenary speakers to add kudos to their events, while charging tens of dollars for attendance but attracting many more delegates as a result. As always, the actual financial consequence of this pivot is unknown, but it is possible some organizers may have not been hit too hard by global lockdowns and may have even benefited from the wholesale shift to online events.

CONFERENCE Q&A

As we approach the end of this overview of predatory publishing, it is worth discussing the predatory conferences alluded to here in terms of how they relate to predatory journals and give an insight into predatory practices. In her article "Learn from my mistakes! What I learned when I spoke at a predatory conference" (Davis, 2021), Colleen Davis relates in excruciating detail how she fell for a predatory conference in 2018. Details of the event included marketing collateral to mimic a legitimate conference and "glossy" brochures including delegates' abstracts. However, there were only a handful of people present, no formal organizer, and other rooms in the venue also included fake events. Davis bravely comes clean about her experiences as a warning to others and shares the following "red flags" about such events:

- Last-minute invitations within a couple of months of the event
- Language used (e.g. English) not at the level expected of an organizer purporting to be from a country where English is the first language
- Being addressed as "Dr." or "Prof." when individuals are not
- Wide variety of disciplines covered—academic conferences are almost always discipline-specific
- As a speaker, being asked to pay for transportation may happen, but rarely to pay for the delegate fee as well

- Requests to speak at events via social media by someone or some organization you are not familiar with should be treated with caution

The detail about the abstracts being published is key as it relates to a common question among researchers: Are predatory conferences linked to predatory journals? The answer is very much "yes." For example, one of the world's most prominent predatory publishers OMICS is also one of the most prominent predatory conference organizers, operating under the OMICS brand and others. OMICS is also thought to run popular conference alert email services, which supply potential delegates details on thousands of conferences around the world, many of which are predatory in nature. As a predatory publisher as well as conference organizer, there are obvious synergies as well when it comes to publishing articles based on speakers' research presentations, meaning that they can either use the lure of speaking at a conference to supply their journals or increase revenues by charging for conference attendance and article publication fees. And as some authors caution, what appears online in the shape of a predatory conference can be difficult to erase (Erdag, 2019).

CONCLUSION

The original aim of this short book was to provide insight into the predatory publishing phenomenon, shining a light onto the shady activities that have caused significant harm in several ways to scholarly communications. We have seen how they developed and have grown, and the agencies that have studied and tried to fight their impact. We have also seen how they can be defined, how they operate, and how authors can mitigate against their activities, as well as how new technology and innovation may be able to minimize their threat.

As a final thought for the future, given the range and variety of tools becoming available for individual researchers, their institutions, and their funders—added to the growing awareness of predatory journals in all disciplines—one would have thought predatory publishers' activities will inevitably decline. However, as Open Access continues to develop as a mode of publishing articles and the "publish or perish" dynamic continues to push authors toward publication, the necessary conditions that have allowed predatory journals to flourish remain. Recent journal hijackings such as that have emerged in Russia (Abalkina, 2021) and improved the standard of journal homepages suggest that predatory publishers may become more sophisticated and adopt new strategies to enable them to exploit the basic publishing model. It is the hope of this book that it encourages the hunted to become the hunters and use the information that has been shared on predatory publishers to avoid their traps and build back the credibility they have stolen from academic research and publishing.

ACKNOWLEDGMENTS

I would like to thank Cabells for their support in writing this book and for providing data from its *Predatory Reports* database. Sincere thanks to my editor at Charleston Briefings Matthew Ismail for his patience and guidance, and to Anthony Watkinson and other reviewers for their invaluable advice on the manuscript.

READING LIST

The following references indicate recommended reading in and around the topic of predatory journals and scholarly communications as a whole.

BOOKS

Anderson, R. (2018). *Scholarly Communication: What Everyone Needs to Know*. Oxford University Press. https://global.oup.com/academic/product/scholarly-communication-9780190639457?cc=gb&lang=en&

Czisar, A. (2018). *The Scientific Journal. Authorship and the Politics of Knowledge in the Nineteenth Century*. The University of Chicago Press. https://press.uchicago.edu/ucp/books/book/chicago/S/bo28179042.html

Greco, A. N. (2020). *The Business of Scholarly Publishing*. Oxford University Press. https://global.oup.com/academic/product/the-business-of-scholarly-publishing-9780190626235?cc=gb&lang=en&

Iphofen, R. (Ed.) (2020). *Handbook of Research Ethics and Scientific Integrity*. Springer. https://link.springer.com/referencework/10.1007/978-3-030-16759-2

Marcum, D. & Schonfeld, R.C. (2021). *Along Came Google: A History of Library Digitization*. Princeton University Press. https://press.princeton.edu/books/hardcover/9780691172712/along-came-google

Poff, D. (2023). *Encyclopaedia of Business and Professional Ethics*. Springer. https://link.springer.com/referencework/10.1007/978-3-319-23514-1

Weller, M. (2011). The Digital Scholar: How Technology is Transforming Scholarly Practice. Bloomsbury. www.bloomsbury.com/uk/digital-scholar-9781849664974/

Xia, J. (2022). *Predatory Publishing*. Routledge. www.routledge.com/Predatory-Publishing/Xia/p/book/9780367465322

WEBSITES

Cabells' The Source blog: https://blog.cabells.com/
COPE website and resources: https://publicationethics.org/
Retraction Watch: https://retractionwatch.com/
The Scholarly Kitchen: https://scholarlykitchen.sspnet.org/

REFERENCES

Abalkina, A. (2021). *Hijacked Journals in Scopus*. ResearchGate. www.researchgate.net/
publication/352062052_Hijacked_journals_in_Scopus

Amrit, B.L.S. (2021, October 29). Bootlegging, Retconning: How Predatory Journals are
Adapting to Scrutiny. *The Wire*. https://science.thewire.in/the-sciences/bootlegging-
retconning-predatory-journals-adapting-scrutiny/

ANSInet. (n.d.). *Journal of Biological Sciences*. ANSInet. Retrieved December 22, 2021, from
https://ansinet.com/jhome.php?issn=1727-3048

Bagues, M., Sylos-Labini, M. & Zinovyeva, N. (2017). Walk on the Wild Side: 'Predatory'
Journals and Information Asymmetries in Scientific Evaluations. *IZA Discussion
Papers*, DP No. 11041, www.iza.org/publications/dp/11041/a-walk-on-the-wild-side-
predatory-journals-and-information-asymmetries-in-scientific-evaluations

Beall, J. (2009). Bentham open. *The Charleston Advisor*, 11(1), 29–32. https://charleston.
publisher.ingentaconnect.com/contentone/ charleston/chadv/2009/00000011/
00000001/art00008

Beall, J. (2010a). "Predatory" open-access scholarly publishers. *The Charleston Advisor*,
11(4), 10–17. www.ingentaconnect.com/ contentone/charleston/chadv/2010/
00000011/00000004/art00005

Beall, J. (2010b). Update: Predatory open-access scholarly publishers. The Charleston
Advisor, 12(1), 50. https://doi.org/10.5260/chara.12.1.50

Beall, J. (2012a). Five scholarly open access publishers. *The Charleston Advisor*, 13(4), 5–10.
https://doi.org/10.5260/chara.13.4.5

Beall, J. (2012b). Predatory publishers are corrupting open access. Nature, 489, 179. www.
nature.com/news/polopoly_fs/1.11385!/menu/main/topColumns/topLeftColumn/
pdf/489179a.pdf

Beall, J. (2012c). Criteria for determining predatory open access publishers. Scholarly OA.
Retrieved January 5, 2022, from https://scholarlyoa.files.wordpress.com/2012/11/
criteria-2012-2.pdf

Beall, J. (2013). The open-access movement is not really about open access. *triple C:
Communication, Capitalism & Critique*, 11(2), 589–597. www.triple-c.at/index.php/
tripleC/article/view/525

Beallslist. (2021). Beall's List. Retrieved June 3, 2021, from https://beallslist.net/

Berlin Declaration. (2003). Berlin Declaration on Open Access to Knowledge in the Sciences and Humanities. Retrieved 5 January, 2022, https://web.archive.org/web/20151027030958/http://openaccess.mpg.de/Berlin-Declaration

Björk, B-C. (2019). Open access journal publishing in the Nordic countries. *Learned Publishing*, 32(3), 227–236. https://onlinelibrary.wiley.com/doi/full/10.1002/leap.1231

Björk, B-C, Kanto-Karvenen, S., &. Harviainen, J.T. (2019). How frequently are articles in predatory open access journals cited. *publications*, 8(2), 17. www.mdpi.com/2304-6775/8/2/17

Budapest Open Access Initiative. (2002). Budapest Open Access Initiative. Retrieved January 6, 2022, from www.budapestopenaccessinitiative.org/read

Bohannon, J. (2013). Who's afraid of peer review?. *Science*, 342(6154), 60–65. www.science.org/doi/abs/10.1126/science.2013.342.6154.342_60

Brembs, B. (2015, October 23). Predatory priorities. Björn.Brembs.Blog. http://bjoern.brembs.net/2015/10/predatory-priorities/

Brembs, B. (2019, December 11). Elsevier now officially a predatory publisher. Björn.Brembs.Blog. http://bjoern.brembs.net/2019/12/elsevier-now-officially-a-predatory-publisher/

Butler, D. (2013). Investigating Journals: the dark side of publishing. Nature, 495, pp. 433–435 www.nature.com/news/investigating-journals-the-dark-side-of-publishing-1.12666

Buryani, S. (2017). Is the staggeringly profitable business of scientific publishing bad for science? The Guardian, 27 Jun., 2017 www.theguardian.com/science/2017/jun/27/profitable-business-scientific-publishing-bad-for-science

Cabells. (n.d.). Predatory Reports. Cabells. Retrieved August 30, 2021, from www2.cabells.com/predatory

Cambridge Dictionary. (n.d.) Accessed 27 May, 2021. https://dictionary.cambridge.org/dictionary/english/predatory

Cobey K.D. (2019). Knowledge and motivations of researchers publishing in presumed predatory journals: a survey. BMJ Open, Vol. 9, Iss. 3, 2019 https://bmjopen.bmj.com/content/9/3/e026516

Collom, C.D., Oermann, M.H., Sabol, V.K. and Heintz, P.A. (2020). An assessment of predatory publication use in reviews. *Clinical Nurse Specialist*, July/August, 2020. https://pubmed.ncbi.nlm.nih.gov/32541600/

Cortegiani A, Ippolito M, Ingoglia G et al. Citations and metrics of journals discontinued from Scopus for publication concerns: the GhoS(t)copus Project [version 2; peer review: 2 approved, 1 approved with reservations]. *F1000Research* 2020, 9:415. https://doi.org/10.12688/f1000research.23847.2

Csiszar, A. (2016). Peer review: Troubled from the start. *Nature* 532, 306–308 (2016). https://doi.org/10.1038/532306a

Crawford, W. (2017). Gray OA 2012–2016: Open Access Journals Beyond DOAJ. Retrieved 10 May, 2022, from http://citesandinsights.info/civ17i1.pdf

Crotty, D. (2018, August 14). Revisiting: Six years of predatory publishing. *Scholarly Kitchen* https://scholarlykitchen.sspnet.org/2018/08/14/revisiting-six-years-predatory-publishing/

Mehdi D., Fariborz R. And Oermann, M.H. (2022) PedCheck: A Dashboard for Analyzing Social Media Posts about Predatory Journals, *Serials Review*, DOI: 10.1080/00987913.2022.2046459

Davis, C. (2021, August 19). Learn from my mistakes! What I learned when I spoke at a predatory conference. *BMJ blog* https://blogs.bmj.com/spcare/2021/08/19/learn-from-my-mistakes-what-i-learned-when-i-spoke-at-a-predatory-conference/

Dell'anno, R., Camera, R. and Morone, A. (2020). A "Trojan Horse" in the peer-review process of fee- charging economic journals. *Journal of Informetrics*, 14.3 (2020) www.sciencedirect.com/science/article/abs/pii/S1751157720300080

Demir, S.B. (2018). Predatory journals: Who publishes in them and why? *Journal of Informetrics, 12.3, www.sciencedirect.com/science/article/abs/pii/S1751157718301962*

Dobusch, L. and Heimstädt, M. (2019). Predatory publishing in management research: A call for open peer review. Management Learning, 50.5, https://journals.sagepub.com/doi/full/10.1177/1350507619878820

Erdag, T.K. (2019). Be aware of predatory/fake conferences!. *Turkish Archives of Otorhinolaryngology*, 57.3, www.ncbi.nlm.nih.gov/pmc/articles/PMC6779098/

Eshchanov,B., Abduraimov, K., Ibragimova, M. and Eshchanov, R. (2019). Efficiency of "Publish or Perish" Policy—Some Considerations Based on the Uzbekistan Experience. *Publications* 9.33. https://doi.org/10.3390/publications9030033

Eykens J., Guns R., Rahman A.I.M.J. and Engels T.C.E. (2019). Identifying publications in questionable journals in the context of performance-based research funding. *PLoS ONE* 14(11). https://doi.org/10.1371/journal.pone.0224541

Eysenbach, G. (2008, August 3). Black sheep among Open Access Journals and Publishers. *Random Research Rants Blog.* http://gunther-eysenbach.blogspot.com

Federal Trade Commission v. Omits Group. Volume F. 152 3113 (2019). www.ftc.gov/enforcement/cases-proceedings/152-3113/federal-trade-commission-v-omics-group-inc

Frandsen, T.F. (2019). Why do researchers decide to publish in questionable journals? A review of the literature. *Learned Publishing* 32: 57–62. https://onlinelibrary.wiley.com/doi/epdf/10.1002/leap.1214

Garfield, E. (2005, September 16). International Congress on Peer Review And Biomedical Publication, http://garfield.library.upenn.edu/papers/jifchicago2005.pdf

Georges, A. (2018, November 5). Dolos list discussion. *ResearchGate.* www.researchgate.net/post/The-Dolos-list-and-the-scientific-community-A-special-relationship

Google Scholar. (n.d.). Google Scholar, Google. Retrieved 30 Jul, 2021, www.scholar.google.com

Greco, A. N. (2020). *The Business of Scholarly Publishing.* Oxford University Press. https://global.oup.com/academic/product/the-business-of-scholarly-publishing-9780190626235?cc=gb&lang=en&

Green, T. (2019). Is open access affordable? Why current models do not work and why we need internet-era transformation of scholarly communications. *Learned Publishing* 32(1) 13–25 https://onlinelibrary.wiley.com/doi/abs/10.1002/leap.1219

Harnad, Stevan (1995) A Subversive Proposal. In, Okerson, A. and O'Donnell, J. (eds.) *Scholarly Journals at the Crossroads: A Subversive Proposal for Electronic Publishing.* Association of Research Libraries, https://eprints.soton.ac.uk/362894/

Hinchliffe, L. (2020). Repairing an Institutional Reputation Tarnished by Fraudulent Publishing. Scholarly Kitchen https://scholarlykitchen.sspnet.org/2019/09/30/repairing-institutional-reputation-fraudulent-publishers/

Indian Journal of Aerospace Medicine (n.d.) Indian Journal of Aerospace Medicine, retrieved 11 May, 2022, https://indjaerospacemed.com/

InterAcademy Partnership. (2022). Combatting predatory academic journals and conferences. www.interacademies.org/project/predatorypublishing

Journal of Industrial Pollution Control. (n.d.) Journal of Industrial Pollution Control. Retrieved 20 June, 2021. www.icontrolpollution.com/

Kendall, G. (2021). Beall's legacy in the battle against predatory publishers. *Learned Publishing*, 34(3) 379–388, https://onlinelibrary.wiley.com/doi/abs/10.1002/leap.1374

Kendall, G. and Linacre, S. (Forthcoming). Predatory Journals: Revisiting Beall's Research. *Publishing Research Quarterly, www.springer.com/journal/12109*

Keough, A. (2020). Beware predatory journals. British Dental Journal, 288, 317. www.nature.com/articles/s41415-020-1374-4

Kimotho, S. (2019). The Storm around Beall's List: A Review of Issues Raised by Beall's Critics over his Criteria of Identifying Predatory Journals and Publishers. African Research Review, 13(1) 1–12, www.researchgate.net/publication/332496019_The_Storm_around_Beall's_List_A_Review_of_Issues_Raised_by_Beall's_Critics_over_his_Criteria_of_Identifying_Predatory_Journals_and_Publishers

Kratochvíl, J., Plch, L., Sebera, M. and Koriťáková, E. (2020). Evaluation of untrustworthy journals: transition from formal criteria to a complex view. Learned Publishing, 33(3), 308–22, https://onlinelibrary.wiley.com/doi/10.1002/leap.1299

Krause, V.T. and Langhans, K. (2018). Tausende Forscher publizieren in Pseudo-Journalen. *Suddeutche Zeitung*. Retrieved 11 Mary, 2022, www.sueddeutsche.de/wissen/wissenschaft-tausende-forscher-publizieren-in-pseudo-journalen-1.4061005

Lenhart, M. (2021). Sham Conferences: Has the Pandemic Made Them Worse?. *Event Manager Blog*. Retrieved Sep 13, 2021. www.eventmanagerblog.com/predatory-conferences.

Likis, F.E. (2019). Predatory Publishing: The Threat Continues. Journal of Midwifery & Women's Health. https://onlinelibrary.wiley.com/doi/full/10.1111/jmwh.13056

Linacre, S. (2020a). A New Year's Resolution Worth Keeping: Say 'NO' to Spam. *The Source*. https://blog.cabells.com/2020/01/15/a-new-years-resolution-worth-keeping-say-no-to-spam/

Linacre, S. (2020b). Cabells' Top 7 Palpable Points About Predatory Publishing Practices. *The Source*. Retrieved, 12 May, 2022. https://blog.cabells.com/2020/07/15/cabells-top-7-palpable-points-about-predatory-publishing-practices/

Linacre, S. (2020c). What to know about ISSNs. *The Source*. Retrieved 12 May, 2022. https://blog.cabells.com/2020/12/02/what-to-know-about-issns/

Linacre, S. (2021a). What Lies Beneath. *The Source*. Retrieved 12 May, 2022. https://blog.cabells.com/2021/08/04/what-lies-beneath-2/

Linacre, S. (2021b). Mountain to Climb. *The Source*. Retrieved 12 May, 2022. https://blog.cabells.com/2021/09/01/mountain-to-climb/

Linacre, S. (2021c). No Signs of Slowing. *The Source*. Retrieved, 12 May, 2022. https://blog.cabells.com/2021/07/07/no-signs-of-slowing/

Linacre, S. (2021d). The Top Nine Questions on Predatory Journals Answered. *The Source*. Retrieved 12 May, 2022. https://blog.cabells.com/2021/06/23/the-top-nine-questions-on-predatory-journals-answered/

Linacre, S., Bisaccio, M. and Earle, L. (2019). Publishing in an Environment of Predation: The Many Things You Really Wanted to Know, but Did Not Know How to Ask. *Journal of Business-to-Business Marketing*, 26(2), 217–228, www.tandfonline.com/doi/full/10.1080/1051712X.2019.1603423

McGlynn, T. (2013). The Evolution of Pseudojournals. *Small Pond Science*. Retrieved 15 May 2022. https://smallpondscience.com/2013/02/14/the-evolution-of-pseudojournals/

McGuigan, G. S. (2004). Publishing Perils in Academe. *Journal of Business & Finance Librarianship*, 10(1), 13–26. www.tandfonline.com/doi/abs/10.1300/J109v10n01_03

Masic, I. (2017). Predatory Publishing—Experience with OMICS International. *Medical Archives*, 71(5). www.ncbi.nlm.nih.gov/pmc/articles/PMC5723186/

Nicholas, D. Jamali, Hamid R. Herman, E., Xu, J.; Boukacem-Zeghmouri, C., Watkinson, A., Rodríguez-Bravo, B., Abrizah, A. Świgoń, M. and Polezhaeva, T. (2020). How is open access publishing going down with early career researchers? An international, multi-disciplinary study. *Profesional de la información*, 29(6). https://doi.org/10.3145/epi.2020.nov.14

Rishi P., M., Patel, V. and Low, G. (2021). Predatory Journals: The Power of the Predator Versus the Integrity of the Honest. Current Problems in Diagnostic Radiology. www.sciencedirect.com/science/article/abs/pii/S0363018821001389

National Academies of Science, Engineering and Medicine. (2021). *Money for Nothing: Predatory Practices in Academic Journals and Conferences*. National Academies of Science, Engineering and Medicine www.nationalacademies.org/event/06-06-2021/money-for-nothing-predatory-practices-in-academic-journals-and-conferences

The Ottowa Hospital Research Institute (2021). Journal Authenticator. Retrieved 28 Oct, 2021. www.ohri.ca/journalology/oss-journal-authenticator

Pagell, R. (2019). Ruth's Rankings 43: Predatory Practices Revisited—Misunderstandings and Positive Actions. *Library Learning Space*. Retrieved 15 May, 2022. https://librarylearningspace.com/ruths-rankings-43-predatory-practices-revisited-misunderstandings-positive-actions/

Jinseo, P., Jinhyuk, Y. and Lee, J. Y. (2019). A Longitudinal Study of Questionable Journals in Scopus. *17th International Conference on Scientometrics & Informetrics*. www.researchgate.net/publication/335715986_A_Longitudinal_Study_of_Questionable_Journals_in_Scopus

Patwardhan, B. (2019). Why India is Striking Back Against Predatory Journals. Nature. www.nature.com/articles/d41586-019-02023-7

Pollock, D. and Michael, A. (2020). News & Views: Open Access Market Sizing Update 2020. *Delta Think*. https://deltathink.com/news-views-open-access-market-sizing-update-2020/

Predatory Publishing. (n.d.). What was the first predatory journal? Who published it? Predatory Publishing. Retrieved June 24, 2021. https://predatory-publishing.com/what-was-the-first-predatory-journal-who-published-it/

Priem, J. [@jasonpriem]. (2020, July 15). *Get this: the MAJORITY (53%) of DOI-assigned articles published in 2019 we #OpenAccess. (I just did saw results of this query on @unpaywall database). That means having to pay to read an article is now THE EXCEPTION, not the rule.* [Tweet]. Twitter. https://twitter.com/jasonpriem/status/1283491796732043265?lang=en

Pyne, D. (2017). The Rewards of Predatory Publications at a Small Business School. *Journal of Scholarly Publishing*, 48(3), 137–160. https://muse.jhu.edu/article/652022

Retraction Watch. (2017). *Retraction Watch*. Retrieved 15 May, 2022. https://retractionwatch.com/2017/01/17/bealls-list-potential-predatory-publishers-go-dark/

Rice, D.B., Skidmore, B. and Cobey, K.D. (2021). Dealing with predatory journal articles captured in systematic reviews. Systematic Reviews. 10(175). https://doi.org/10.1186/s13643-021-01733-2

Rhode, S., Linacre, S. and Berryman, K. (2022). *Hidden dangers: Covid-19-based research in predatory journals.* [Manuscript in preparation].

Salehi, M., Solatani, M., Tamleh, H. and Teirmornezhad, A. (2019). Publishing in predatory open access journals: Authors' perspectives. *Learned Publishing*, 33(2), 89–95 https://onlinelibrary.wiley.com/doi/10.1002/leap.1261

Sanderson, K. (2010). Two new journals copy the old. *Nature*, 463 (7278), 148. https://doi.org/10.1038/463148a

Schira, H.R. and Hurst, C. (2019). Hype or Real Threat: The Extent of Predatory Journals in Student Bibliographies. *Partnership: The Canadian Journal of Library and Information Practice and Research*, 19(1). https://journal.lib.uoguelph.ca/index.php/perj/article/view/4764

Scopus Content Coverage Guide (2020). Scopus. Retrieved 12 December 2021. www.elsevier.com/__data/assets/pdf_file/0007/69451/Scopus_ContentCoverage_Guide_WEB.pdf

Seethapathy, G. S., Santhosh Kumar, J. U. and Hareesha, A. S. (2016). India's scientific publication in predatory journals: need for regulating quality of Indian science and education. *Current Science*, 111(11), 159–1764. www.currentscience.ac.in/Volumes/111/11/1759.pdf

Shamseer, L. (2021). *"Predatory" journals: an evidence-based approach characterising them and considering where research ought to be published.* [PhD thesis, University of Ottawa]. uO Research https://ruor.uottawa.ca/bitstream/10393/41858/1/Shamseer_Larissa_2021_thesis.pdf

Shen, C., Björk, B.C., (2015). 'Predatory' open access: a longitudinal study of article volumes and market characteristics. *BMC Med* 13(230). https://doi.org/10.1186/s12916-015-0469-2

Siler,K., Vincent-Lamarre, P., Sugimoto, C. and Lavriere, V. (2021). Predatory publishers' latest scam: bootlegged and rebranded papers. *Nature*, 598, 563–565. www.nature.com/articles/d41586-021-02906-8

De Silva, J.A.T. (2013).Predatory Publishing. A Quantative Assessment, the Predatory Score. *The Asian and Australasian Journal of Plant Science and Biotechnology*. 7(1), 21–34. www.researchgate.net/publication/283719165_Predatory_Publishing_A_Quantitative_Assessment_the_Predatory_Score

De Silva, J.A.T. (2017). Preprints: ethical hazard or academic liberation? *Kome—An International Journal of Pure Communication Inquiry*, 5(2), 73–80. http://komejournal.com/files/KOME_JATdSpreprints.pdf

De Silva, J.A.T., Dunleavy, D.J., Moradzadeh, M. and Eykens, J. (2021). A credit-like rating system determine the legitimacy of scientific journals and publishers. *Scientometrics*, 126(10), 8589–8616. https://pubmed.ncbi.nlm.nih.gov/34421155/

Statista. (2021). Statista. Retrieved 16 May 2022. www.statista.com/statistics/420391/spam-email-traffic-share/

Stop Predatory Journals (n.d.) Stop Predatory Journals. Retrieved 22 July 2021. https://predatoryjournals.com/

Strinzel, M., Severin, A., Liz, K., and Egger, M. (2019). Blacklists and Whitelists to Tackle Predatory Publishing. A Cross-Sectional Comparison and Thematic Analysis. *mBio*. 10(3). https://journals.asm.org/doi/full/10.1128/mBio.00411-19

Suber, P. (2012). *Open Access Overview*. Retrieved 20 July 2021. https://legacy.earlham. edu/~peters/fos/overview.htm

Tennant, J.P. et al (2019). Ten Hot Topics Around Scholarly Publishing. *Publications* 7(34). www.mdpi.com/2304-6775/7/2/34

Trejo-Pech, C.O., Tis hach, S.V., Thompson, J.M. and Manley, J. (2021). Violations of Standard Practices by Predatory Economics Journals. *Serials Review*, 47(2). www.tandfon line.com/doi/abs/10.1080/00987913.2021.1959183?tab=permissions&scroll=top

Tsigaris, P. And Da Silva, J.A.T. (2019). Did the Research Faculty at a Small Canadian Business School Publish in "Predatory" Venues? This Depends on the Publishing Blacklist. *Publications*, 7(2), 35. www.mdpi.com/2304-6775/7/2/35

University of California. (2019). UC terminates subscription with world's largest publisher in push for open access to publicly funded research. *University of California*. Retrieved 16 May 2022. www.universityofcalifornia.edu/press-room/uc-terminates-subscrip tions-worlds-largest-scientific-publisher-push-open-access-publicly

University Grants Commission. (2021). *University Grants Commission*. Retrieved 16 May 2022. https://ugccare.unipune.ac.in/apps1/home/index

Wikipedia. (2021a). Academic Journal. *Wikipedia*. Retrieved 27 May 2021. https://en.wiki pedia.org/wiki/Academic_journal

Wikipedia. (2021b). Who's afraid of peer review? *Wikipedia*. Retrieved 15 October 2021. https://en.wikipedia.org/wiki/Who%27s_Afraid_of_Peer_Review%3F

Wiley Online Library. (n.d.) *Wiley Online Library*. Retrieved 29 Jun 2021. https://online library.wiley.com/journal/19394225

Yeo-Teh N.S.L and Tang B.L. (2021). Wilfully submitting to and publishing in predatory journals—a covert form of research misconduct? *Biochem Med (Zagreb)*, 31(3) https:// pubmed.ncbi.nlm.nih.gov/34393593/

Yeoh, M., Cazan, A-M., Muss, W. H. Jacic, L. and Zaib, S. (2017). Ethical and Predatory Publishing: Experiences and Perceptions of Researchers. Bulletin of the Transylvania University of Brasov. 10(59 No: 2), 55–70. www.researchgate.net/publication/ 321875076_Ethical_and_predatory_publishing_Experiences_and_perceptions_of_ researchers